THE GLASS PIANO

Ben Mazer

MADHAT PRESS
ASHEVILLE, NORTH CAROLINA

MadHat Press
MadHat Incorporated
PO Box 8364, Asheville, NC 28814

Copyright © 2015 Ben Mazer
All rights reserved

The Library of Congress has assigned
this edition a Control Number of
2015917314

ISBN 978-1-941196-22-9 (paperback)

Text by Ben Mazer
Cover photograph by Allison Vanouse
Cover design and art by Marc Vincenz

www.MadHat-Press.com

First Printing

THE GLASS PIANO

CONTENTS

Lupe Velez with a Baedeker: Irving Thalberg with a Cigar	1
Andante	2
Autumn Magazines	3
My Last Dutchman	4
"The stars are icy in the sky"	9
"One dresses in the darkened gloom"	10
"Spread over the vast sinking town"	11
Intimations	12
October Garden	15
The Heart	16
Starlight by Streetlight	17
"I shall not need your arms in heaven,"	19
"The windmills turn, but no one can push back the wind."	20
"Tonight my lover lies"	21
Delirium	23
"When it hails in the morning, I remember,"	24
"Why is it some old magazine, like a wheelbarrow,"	25
"The poet does his finest work in sin,"	26
Spring	27
"In summer I coil in my serpent's nest,"	28
"Things are what they seem to be awhile;"	29
"Which crazy mental patient are you?"	30
"Autumn for the people and the favorable island"	31
The Years in Switzerland	32

"When she is lying in her grave," 33
"The pristine blues and greens of waving" 34
"The brilliance of lost days surrounds the night," 35
"Strange that all the people that you meet" 36
"Meanwhile you come to me with vipers' eyes" 37
"So in the recent arms of memory" 38
"Time wrecks them, but despite time they persist." 39
"No longer discerning between the snow and sea," 40
"The last stop, the seventeenth century:" 41
"The smaller ego is so infinite," 42
"We sit in Central Park, the awful dark" 43
"Night. We stand beneath a thousand stars," 44
"Home was the place I knew night after night," 45
"And now each place I walk like one who's dead," 46
Une Chienne Masonique
    dans la grande lavatoire oceanographique 47
"The clouds are gathered," 51
Missing Persons 52
Spring Frost 53
"Gradually the house across the way" 54
The Place 57
Winnie's Tower 58
"Graves and waves are signified by rows," 59
Brown Hours 60
"Supreme the snows make compacts of our youth," 61
"Shing-tu would wander daily to the wharves;" 62

"The general had his coffee on the terrace,"	63
"I aspired to be mad like him,"	64
"He sauntered briskly on the tennis court,"	65
The Glass Piano	66
"Alone, who loved her, held in high esteem,"	68
A New-Fangled Prodigal	69
"Grandma Florence went riding over the hills,"	71
	72
Double Plot	76
"High alcoves, orange walls rising to the night"	78
"To look at them, who moved so easily"	80
Poem	81
"Tear away, oh tear away the veil"	82
"The idle roofs are slags and crags"	83
The Styrofoam Clown	84
The Golden Pear	86
"When like a perjured idiot I ran"	87
"To go back now, is to relinquish trust"	88
Trees	90
"The visible soda shop, arresting form,"	91
"I moved through my huge family's world,"	92
"I saw her once, I don't know where I was"	93
"The sea is no longer the sea,"	96
	98
"I tried to find you in that surging mob"	101

Thirties Poem	102
Berryman at Columbia	103
"'Twas then I knew the meaning of the sea,"	104
"Greens dark and light of evergreen and fir"	105
Word	106
Gesture	106
"Perhaps some one of you has lost a friend,"	107
"When memory depletes, a slow peace comes"	108
"These highways littered with the oxes skulls,"	109
Bix Beiderbecke (1903–1931)	110
A Pastoral Interjection	111
"When we were young, our poetry shot stars"	112
"Words are just words"	113
Holy Sonnet	115
Skiing After Nazis in Ottawa	116
"The sun was shining, and the yucca-yuk"	118
"Our logic will not seem to do"	119
"I also can recall distinct sensation"	120
"And when I look upon the moon"	121
"And what comes after? Let there be a daughter"	122
"The car sweeps round the curves and winding lanes"	123
"Imagined grandeur covets and conceals"	124
"The little girl who stumbles like a hen"	125
"The mantel clock"	126
"In spring a strange pervasive smell persists,"	127

Meditations	129
"Flat planes"	132
"The newspapers are rows of plotted fields"	133
"A black man sleeps inside a dusty cellar;"	134
"Lewis is dead. Retinal Imperialist,"	135
"It was on a grey rainy day,"	136
"Blown on the widow walk she holds"	137
"There is no perfect synthesis,"	139
Necesse est Perstare?	140
An After Dinner Sleep	143
Afterword: Ben Mazer Interviewed by Robert Archambeau	157
About the Author	170

The Glass Piano

Lupe Velez with a Baedeker: Irving Thalberg with a Cigar

The smoky candle end of time
declines. On the Rialto once.
With Lupe Velez. Prepared the crime.
But Irving's valet was no dunce.

Had seen Tirolean dances there
before. And though she was no whore.
Perhaps was hired by the state.
Yet would not scare. And knew no fate.

Time's thick castles ascend in piles,
the witnesses to countless mobs.
Each with intentions, torches, throbs.
Bequeath the coming dawn their wiles.

Yet Irving was not meant for this.
He books the first flight to the States.
He suffers to receive Lupe's kiss.
While all around the chorus prates.

There's something does not love a mime.
Tirolean castles built to scale.
There was a mob. There is no crime.
These modernisms sometimes fail.

Ben Mazer

Andante

All is flux and change, Lucretius said.
These gardens are kept manicured. This bed
is cradled high among the well-trimmed trees
that branch off into shadows, and waver in the breeze.
Night spotlights young girls' impulses to flee
where drunken bushes have the best of me.
Familiar songs blare distantly one face,
yet there are others hidden, beneath the human race.
A dim potato sprouts beneath the soil.
At summer solstice we retire from toil,
and settling in among the verdant reach
of shapes and colors find, observance in the breach.
There is no one to tell us what to do.
The driven many emulate the few,
and tearing away memory like veils
report internally, the iconry of tales.
One leaves one's life, to instigate another.
He is no brother, she no longer mother.
The unimaginable at last comes true.
And there is nothing left, and nothing left to do.
The heart is still, admiring pink roses,
no longer shaken by years' monstrous doses.
Somewhere all begins again anew,
and there is nothing left, and nothing left to do.

Autumn Magazines

The falling leaves of autumn magazines
are framed by nature. Frost said you come too.
Your gowns and sandals crown your nakedness,
each season justifies all that you do.
The sidewalks spread out their appearances,
the towers and the gilding celebrate
the dates and calendars, commemorate,
and underneath it all there's only you.

Ben Mazer

My Last Dutchman

I do not need historical accuracy
to be who I am. My window's little view
admits an occasional passing ball or girl
amidst the flowers that I call my own.
My people were Dutch or French, that painter Hals
was one of them. I keep one on my walls
as a sort of a conversation piece,
though strictly conversation's not my forte.
In France now Mesmerism is the rage;
they say Franz Anton Mesmer is a sage,
he took Ben Franklin up in a balloon;
but what is that to me, who have confined
myself to gardens here on this estate?
In youth I pined for new philosophy,
and sought to find it in the weekly papers.
But now, in the decrepit rancour of my age,
confined by gout and palsy to my bed,
I more and more retreat into my head,
or take my pleasure looking out of windows.
I who cannot imagine the living Tyre,
or trace the etymology of language.
A girl passed this way several days ago,
who must have chased a cat into the garden.
I saw her at the window's very edge,
or part of her. The whole view was occluded,
being in motion and too far to one side.
A leg, a dress, some laughter and some talk,
meant for the cat no doubt. While I inside
struggled to glimpse the colour of her hair.
Her feet were very white and pink and bare,

and auburn gold the colour of her hair.
I counted the minutes till I saw her eyes,
so dark blue-green they filled me with surprise.
She couldn't have been much more than eleven.
I knew a woman once who was of age,
and watched her so, while reading books. I spied.
Yet even then, though my view were occluded
I wanted to see her partially denuded,
and wondered should I let her glimpse of me?
What were the likelihood that she could see?
Or hear. Then a strict panic took me back.
First thought. No, that can't be correct.
It is legitimate to inspect
the frames of windows.
Looking outward is my first ambition.
I have not the learning or cognition
to sense of this her burning rampart plums,
twizzling once as though to prove Weslier's theory.
Cool bath pools, limestone quarries, clock my mind.
I have gathered these tomes to one side,
grouping them accordingly as one author,
the history of an age inherited.
Chiefly such terminologies have swept Europe
briefly in images, glanced in the corner of talk,
like the voice of the oboe over the orchestra,
inevitably superseded by voices of friends,
extinguished in the ocean of recognized consciousness.
Look at their jackets. Something is very different about each one.
Six years of monthlies that I paid to bind.
Angels are visitors to different houses.
They are transparent, yet to the mind are white.

Ben Mazer

While to other people, even cousins,
they are real people. Their voices in houses
(and hear I cannot escape my own)
allay fears with ordinary transactions.
Cousins are humourous, good to have in the house.
I want to go everywhere with Fred, or be alone with Roger.
Julia and Jennifer are my spies in court.
I have hung mirrors on lengthy poles
to catch a glimpse of my aunt undressing in the room next to mine,
for several days through the spring festivals,
or was it the harvest. Night of the thunderstorm.
To have come from far places tired, garrulous.
The crisp decree of history in the air,
harsh like the talk of the viceroy, her husband,
who beat us all at cards, but gave us cheroots,
but a dull monotone spread over the western world
as far along the calendar's divide
to China as any theory of gravity.
It hung in the air like Franklin in his balloon,
at night I hope it was, Franklin and Mesmer talking,
for upwards is space that is continuous with issued thought.

The development of nations is nothing to the
absolute apostle who rides the throne at the center.
Hermetic I should loan her to her mother.
Begin to understand one voice speaks for the nation,
it is what we take home with our hearts.
It is the voice of time and space and science,
which co-exists with Africa and Japan.
I have spent days in the gardens or at the zoo,
and felt that I could travel anywhere.

But to be leaving, by train or by ship,
carries with it a sense that is thunderous,
not merely the joy of being with family,
but the dark pleasure obstructed by distance and mountains,
the true lightning and lightning rod of the age.
It is the gods still that we beckon to.
It is something we all know. What is it?
The voice of the ocean. The thunder. The atmosphere.
Trading an ever rolling algorithm of series of numbers
on the market, welcoming a January day.
It is the dull tolling of time at the end of death,
and the likelihood of other people before here like us.
But it is the firm reply of trade, and the wealth of nations,
the hum of the shell that stretches across dreams
and tidies up each hour of the night,
till pennies are different than minutes count,
or the stroke of the waltz under rapid feet.
We hug, we say good night, we the elite.
There isn't any stroke in dreams of wars.
Far different and far distant a reach.
None are isolated in careers.
Probably France could tell you. My reply
is a firm faith in the lord Jesus, though I go to no churches.
I practice certain services at home, by correct light,
with a simple faith. Contrive of midnight
the alchemical ulterior of day's brisk schedule,
and remember the dead. My little window
breathes the faith light of the Virgin Mary,
dandelion puffballs blown across the summer.

Ben Mazer

Far east of the north corridor
stand certain mountains of the Himalayas.
By these you may tell a diver's pearl in Subu,
or exhaust the eyes of day in winter,
sure of a woman's obedience, the lord
of pregnant familiars. The vast waste
is idle too, obedient to these powers.
Decrees and universal knowledge fill the hours.

But that day when I faced her living sex
there was no way of getting round it.
She preferred me to all other men.
I was compelled to repay the compliment.
That is an old book. I could look it up.
There beside the first assessment of modern psychology.
I worked for no wage.
Women, as we Dutch say, were all over me.

The Glass Piano

The stars are icy in the sky
My senses blinded by the snow
A single lantern burns, prevails
But I don't know which way to go
All houses have been put to bed
And snow is melting on my head
The snow is falling steadfastly
The mirror of eternity
What is supposed will live again
In winter warmth of houses when
The silver gleams and cashmere seams
Falling to earth and winter dreams
Desire creeps down darkened halls
Examines etches on the walls
By charcoal light the windows screen
By half-light where the past is seen
And some young maiden in her thrall
Is wanting to go in the hall
She listens quietly in bed
To the commandments of the head
The lord of the corporeal
But I am lost, directionless
And passed this way an hour ago
The numbers have no sequences
Are quickly covered up by snow

One dresses in the darkened gloom
of winter mornings in one's room
Enlivened to arrive at school
Wet coats are hanging in the hall
Adults inhabit offices
Each dreaming of December's kiss
When all true loves capitulate
Before the hour grows too late
The television keeps us warm
And houses keep us far from harm
Surrounded by one's family
Know visions of eternity
To be a part of what goes on
Even while dressing in the dawn

The Glass Piano

Spread over the vast sinking town
Which winter makes seem half asleep
A bus begins its movement down
Across a bridge into the steep
Wide view of the familiar sights
The site of many rowdy nights
But now inhabitants have thinned
Discouraged by the winter wind
And one less one is in the world
Because our faith and will have curled
And folded on the mantel bare
To leave unborn without a care
One whom God's glory wanted there

Ben Mazer

Intimations

I

Rows of deserted mannequins
are capturements of sleep's desire
along the late night avenue
where the small wishes soon retire
in slanted shadows of the lights
that shade into the memory
of similar imagined nights
along some other destiny—
the perfumes, and the costume pearls,
the feathered hats, a cashmere shawl,
accoutrements of other girls,
all comb the speculative hall
of minor satisfactions sent
to heaven's darkened wonderment.

II

You see it from some other way,
perhaps adjoined to panes of ice
across some kitchen's verity,
who pay not the required price—
god's eye of anonymity
encinctured ocean passages
to fell sleep's closed eternity
and stifle darkness with a kiss …
The shards of fragmented approach
will be swept up when giants come
all other years to swiftly broach
your simple, broad elysium—

and tender a swift word or smile
of stippled presences awhile.

III

This violet sort of calendar
scuttles desire which is sent
where the October winds concur
on every orphan exilement—
the muffled shoes beat down the street
to join each lofty ornament
that sizes sleepers up discrete
along each sullen bafflement;
each exiled casement of the sense
entinctures trinkets in the hand
to ask one perfect recompense,
one seedbed spread across the land
in sleep... Now fold the newspaper,
all mythic quarries to aver.

IV

Then finally, swept into the slant
of closing wishes to decant
some semblance of the tablature
perennial only to the time
of crying eyes that glide the mirror
of steady junctures seized in rime...
each signal imprint of pure form
upsets the census of the norm,
belies some craft's indifference...

Ben Mazer

Stand tall and striding thus framed hence
project some future to recall
the blistered marble of the sense,
and hang your hat up in the hall,
one integer and protocol.

October Garden

Pine swells, garden beds of yellow leaves
below where vacant footsteps crumple light
the surrogate of night air crisply blows
to no one ... Stand now ready for descent
into the garden, words the body meant
to still the soul and amplify desire ...
One cold and crypto-temporal fall pyre
of abstract voices, climbing the stair higher ...
Tell me, is this what you mean or meant
when in October you came at my call
like certain ghosts, to be in love, in thrall ...
You are my guide. The world spins from its center,
we reach the door, we knock, and then we enter ...
To be alive, as oceans born of clocks
or radios transmute the distant docks
into the shadow of a window blind,
and slats of light that rectify the mind,
can't put it right ... yet leave alone the wind.

Ben Mazer

The Heart

Silently the projector burned …
Flown over the lights of the world,
one juncture transatlantically hurled …
Your place in time, expedient and sound,
incomprehensible, inscrutable …
one crossing flash of lights … The world is round …
The world one ball, desire and ambition …
The silver screen still flickering in contrition …
From oceans upwards, then to reach the ground …
Eternal love, concise without a sound …
To drop me here … in history's great rush …
with your eyes only to dispel the crush …
Two little people, yet shall all the world
slyly about their consciousness be curled.
The world conspired to establish Paris,
the striding figure of Sebastian Harris …
whose hat band gleams, reflected in a window …
Dashing and impeccable … Que lindo …
But he is but a rumour to me now …
Some clippings, and a clipper … Tell me how
the flowers of our civilization rise
to their perfection, when the Phoenix dies …
While stacks of Eiffel Towers on a shelf
all gleam in plated gold, and pick up dust …
Someone must remember, someone must …
The Queen Mary bellows, takes a bow …
These things are idle rumours to me now …

The Glass Piano

STARLIGHT BY STREETLIGHT

October is tinted green, blue, violet, tan,
to accommodate the pedestrian,
who leaves the starlight of the city's windows,
to wander past the shops that evenings close,
on his way home, beneath the roaring el,
where leaves swirl in the air, this side of hell.
A million visages, a million words,
of advertising copy, conversations
heard in the street, or heard in railway stations,
invade the heart, informing its desire
for privacy, for lying in the dark,
and emanating magically higher,
up through the tinted light, the falling leaves,
high up past violet Venus's lone spark,
where moonlight settles on the snow-white eves
of certain quaint restrictions, four mute walls,
the in between state of the darkened halls:
to say, I'm mine. I am the one I am.
Let Archimedes fall on swift, dull Priam.
Let stars be rockets, stir audible Tyre.
The glittering mastodon is all for hire,
and Jesus speaks, and Franklin, and Rousseau,
illuminated there, with piercing echo.
Spread out across the vagrant orchard trees,
the cellar that the spider only sees,
with apple smells, an Indian Summer breeze,
alerts the senses, lone in supposition
of ecstasy in very high position.
But Dante goes. The orange trees are too real,
to hope exemplify the nuptial peal

of separate strangers, who align in tenses,
past tick tock clocks that time the sleeping senses.
The morning shall stand proud, lit in the hall,
or huddling on street corners, clutching bundles,
a brokerage of lassitude and thrall,
of portraits on a terra cotta wall,
beside the phone that rings and shakes the candy,
the pencils and the paper that are handy.
The day is jubilant, and all are free,
to ice skate in the park, or sit beneath a tree,
although we meet back here for lunch at three.
Never mind that dinner is at seven,
or that each one aspires to his own heaven.
Let darkness gather round the radio;
let each feel all, but tell not what they know.
The world war has begun. Just so. Just so.

I shall not need your arms in heaven,
nor gem-light singular of your eyes,
before I come to six or seven,
to lure me with much keener lies.

I shall not need your legs in heaven,
you dangled bonny by my side,
but forward all things shall be riven,
eternity we shall abide.

I shall not use your eyes in heaven
to steer me forth into the sun,
but as when conversation's done,
shall be unto the darkness given.

Ben Mazer

       i.m. Seamus Heaney 1939–2013

The windmills turn, but no one can push back the wind.
It comes from the far darkness, and without a sound
war drops confetti primers where the young will find
the haw beds stirring, laughing where great words resound.
The spires of the citadel are stark and bare,
no longer young, none striding forth with prospects there
to find the mazy streets lead to the fulsome world …
for darkness once again has been to darkness hurled.
A great one's passed, who validated much of youth …
to rattle in the darkness, finding signs of truth.
His clear voice boomed and worked to put us all at ease
with prospects of a keen, perpetual increase.
Now we shall hear his voice no more, except in signs
the sharp and shaping anvil has its grand designs.

The Glass Piano

Tonight my lover lies
like a package in my arms,
through skylight darkened skies
and not yet future harms,
surrounded by the stars,
and everything seems sad,
the lover unfulfilled,
the dying in their tears,
the long sad mystery
of your allotted years;
where have the others gone
who were so lean and kind,
so much you can't recall,
so much you'll never find,
a feeling's left when you
have put them out of mind;
I walk out for a smoke,
sit by the garden wall,
the crooked old fence smiles,
the vines are drenched with time,
their shadows hang like loves
and lives beyond your ken;
the smallest place of night
will never come again;
the vintages of years
have bubbled up again;
they hang drenched in the dew,
forgotten summer nights,
with nothing left to do
far from the teeming sights

Ben Mazer

of day and men and rue
the failing of the lights.

Delirium

I hear my mother rattling in the sink,
though I am loose in dreamy marble halls,
my sense of time is present, and I think
that comfort ravages the castle walls.
Night is as tall as those who are within
should wish to speak, of anything at all,
with fever burning underneath the skin,
to whom infinity could be so small.
I fall to earth in my delirium,
and wake to life to find I'm being shot
by someone who was real but now is not,
a skinny robber, canceling out the sum.
Dad's in his parka in the cold garage;
I'm strangely comforted by this barrage.

Ben Mazer

When it hails in the morning, I remember,
while others aren't up, before dawn,
the emotions of other people walking
in earlier decades, in time that is gone.
Why is it the striking hail,
rattling like thoughts at the window,
swept up by the perpetual wind
in the groaning echo of the showering years,
should fix a fine point of conversation
between two conspirators on the wasted plane,
into a pattern, a brocaded tapestry,
of obsolescence, trailing about the heart.

Why is it some old magazine, like a wheelbarrow,
lies rusted, barely out of sight, from the window
a reminder of stragglers drifting through the green,
where a statue of Cromwell interests an April robin.
Do they break to partake of a layered cake and tea
in the Queen's old inn (let things be relative),
powdering their uniforms with the immediacy of thought,
so darkly green, amidst the ephemeral sawdust,
or can it be that some graduating class,
feeling the roots stirring beneath the soil,
should enter the text and conversation of man,
with no deterrent, both royally and hopeful.

Ben Mazer

The poet does his finest work in sin,
travelling across the world to kill his love,
real beauty's on the outside looking in,
at what each year spring to the pollen does,
at tides of granite whirling to new cause,
new steadiments aligning to new pause,
but love is heated by the same old sun,
true beauty's on the outside looking in.
The noon's bazaar, with hazing to be won,
indifference to how each customer ticks,
they flood the streets of Sydney, or are done
with dust for cafe by the blow of six,
the main thing is protect the potato bin,
on this assignment, outside looking in.

Suppose she falters, crushed between the hand
like paper that a flame extinguishes,
let rice and poppies blow across the land
to sing her praises, buried with the fishes,
time's truth is darkness, and the dark is vicious,
even poets must confess their sin,
observing Christmas dinner from the bushes,
a pas de trois, and outside looking in.
The punts of April chafe Ophelia,
pierced by a silver Buddha on a pin;
who splits the spectrum will contrive to steal you;
and though no greater beauty come again,
and blaze like towers while the absent spin,
let God himself be outside looking in.

Spring

The slender nymph dips toward the slender pool,
but I am not that way. The dark scar harms.
Tell me about Europe and her charms.
Leave ruined cities for another day,
and come out where the evening's bright and cool.
The festival, you've got to pay and pay.
No, I am not complete. My contracts say
that I shall be required to play the fool,
that rice is meat, that anything at all
might be my intellectual property.
The glass piano falters on the wall.
I thumb my roses at the Medici,
and quiver like a web at Botticelli.
The earth emerges fresh and clean in spring.
Disorder is the beauty of the thing.

In summer I coil in my serpent's nest,
and read Anne Dick was in the Hound & Horn
(she wasn't); I no longer hope for rest,
the brood's pride, castling among the oaks,
untethered, phrases from emotions torn.
Like an old couple, we sit by the docks
an hour or two, objectiveless, and worn,
considering the many summers spent
dodging parlours, stopping to attest
the glint of sunlight on a well wrought rail.
How many courtyards, places we have stood,
ebb in the fierce desire to procure
some form of permanence that needn't fail,
a way of loving which is always good.

The Glass Piano

Things are what they seem to be awhile;
the towers stand, De Kooning's in the turnstile;
the price of medicine eclipses towns
you've never heard of, a thousand wrinkled frowns;
but we have walked this April day in Autumn,
past all our scenes, with senses awakening
at intervals and hours that we know,
each duly appointed on the itinerary
of the concrete and fragile private museum
of going home, steadfast, traditional;
no one is here to wake us from our dream;
the colors were brilliant, the cornices stood out,
their shadows opportunities, the smells
of nascent flowers steady to the touch
not what we'd noticed in our long retreat,
commemorative to the touch and smell;
the many angles of our flailing arms
in doubled talk, in imitative walk,
sink through the heart that knows biography;
all day we feast our eyes on what we see,
and close the evening on our old familiars.

Ben Mazer

Which crazy mental patient are you?
I'm Robert Lowell. I have no particular goal
except to fool the doctors here and there.
I like to act as if I do not care,
and chop up art with razor blades, and then
confound all issues with the question when.
Now, they say, but now is not the time
the building scattered as the bricks all fell,
the time that I grew intimate with hell,
what's more, now isn't the pervasive swirl
of absences. The bedsheets make the girl
when it comes time for group theatricals.
The intern stands beside me and he pulls
hard on the hem of my espaliers.
My knowledge slides to light, and I feel worse.
Left over gargoyles watch and are our curse.

Autumn for the people and the favorable island
is steadfast while the warriors carve out
a new aesthetic, a distinct attitude,
changes in spirit which are arbitrary.
The old clock ticking on the mantel still,
the love letters, commemorative matches,
uphold the rains while steadily encroach
the different systems of newfangled aims.
Distinctions parsed out to the Indian cliffs
are not the inevitable consequence
of historical pressures, but interchangeable
with personalities of equal flair;
at base these manifestations are psychotic.
A mottled history of starts and ends
fades with the summer, to be taken up
in infancy by providential readers.

Ben Mazer

The Years in Switzerland

Grids of windows, endless across the way,
soaked in a rainstorm, compress the world
to loss and distance, necessary silences
that swell to voices in the imagination.
Beyond the visit, light of the kitchen's glare
peered into from an angel gargoyle rain,
she sweeps insistently the kitchen floor
and feeds the cats with a perpetual care—
we are alone, safe haven with a door.
Pasta fills jars, the papers on the table
are not the same as every other home's—
you being there. But I am fragmented forever.
I've lost my orders, and I have no center.
Only the things I wanted, history,
have withered by my side, knowledge quite useless
without a throughline. I've miscalculated.
The steady ring of gold was once a boat
which crossed the rooftop. Blissful poverty!
In and out of every seafood stand
for years, admit the fireworks on the shoreline
contained one perfect element of love.
This is refused me now. But we can talk,
shyly, with hurtful silences, all lost
that was for years our only sacred dowry.

When she is lying in her grave,
no other men will know what silence gave
to the wind waving all the tops of trees,
to the snow falling on the empty seas,
how she in silence would surmise
eternal death that lurked behind men's eyes,
how words would seize
the visages of memory that flees;
she is so still, that lying there
myself am prone to utter disrepair
to have loved, and seen my true love flown
to silences that I have never known,
to distances where all is reconvened,
not shattered by time's heartless lying fiend.

Ben Mazer

The pristine blues and greens of waving
palms and fronds and stiff perennials
inutterable in silence yet are saving,
where memory like a cool liquid falls
upon my head to break my absence leaving.
So still, the princess temple Diokhu
reminds me of letters she was writing, who
extinguishes the distances of breathing,
knowing no more the palpable senses' core,
the diver's yearning, or the open door
into the isolating paradise
of earthly time that looked into her eyes,
having no purpose left, to put away
even this garden for eternity.

The Glass Piano

The brilliance of lost days surrounds the night,
shining in abstraction, for what is real
and most particular has taken flight—
a putting away of all the things we feel.
The sheets of virgin snow that know no end,
climbing past windows to eternity—
there is no temporality to mend
the blotted out lives that the eye can't see;
the sea! The brilliant light of being there,
whole for a time, believing we exist,
exulting, sharing what the heart's laid bare,
not yet in darkness where all things are missed.
Where is their closure for the heart's desire,
except in instant death, all tightly sealed,
the famous city abandoned with its choir,
the true and only love at last revealed.

Ben Mazer

Strange that all the people that you meet
seem so replete, so complete;
you meet them once again, their charms repeat
until their obsolescence cools the midnight street
and zig-zag wanderings down to the sea
where only thoughts of you and me
align the stars or shoot across the sky
past high-trimmed hedges' silhouetted edges
with little reports of how we too will die.
The moonlight dredges
the bottoms of the pools of memory
yet cannot see
the moving company that our fates direct
to put our lives in storage after all is wrecked.

The Glass Piano

Meanwhile you come to me with vipers' eyes
to ask, Is there one among us who never dies?
I look into the bottom of my pack of lies
and answer, The Phoenix, though Lord knows she sometimes tries.
You take my answer in your sort of stride,
and once again the stars align and ride
into our lives, upon the carpeted floor,
and the high mantle where you look no more
for evidence of what has gone before;
all stammers slightly,
and the evening closes up its door,
wrong or rightly; colorfully and brightly
some vestiges or trace of memory
falls on the wall; you close your eyes to see.

Ben Mazer

So in the recent arms of memory
one image holds; one vast and endless sea
of virgin snowflakes spreading from the Pole,
burying calendars; each in his hole
or swift compartment held in the sky aloft
the levels spreading to eternity,
thinks of his global opposite, some croft
where all is buried, while the anchoring tree
of individual desire, which has doffed
its hat and cape, and spread out all its things
time harnesses residually, and sings
softly stern branch, swift flake, winds' rustlings
into the well-worn depths and roots that ring
the sensibilities to which they cling.

The Glass Piano

Time wrecks them, but despite time they persist.
The sealed compartments that the eye has missed,
stacked high and climbing to eternity;
emblems of blindness that the eye will see.
Wittgenstein said to keep a respectful silence,
who understood the cataclysmic violence
of knowledge, verging metaphysical;
no matter if the vacant parlour wall
should steer a glassed-in clown's face to the all
of passing headlights, private indecisions
time wrecks; their verisimilitude will fall,
and all the substance of the inner visions.
One came this way, with leaves blown when it was fall;
but now the winter makes its cold incisions.

Ben Mazer

No longer discerning between the snow and sea,
I contemplate what you have meant to me,
a kind of resonance of my own thoughts,
the very substance of the imagination;
the devil carves our memory in lots,
and forces us to eat our own abrasion;
I rise till dawn, then fold the walls I use
to covet voices till they are abstruse;
you sleep, but with your permanence assured;
I am a dunce, the winter has me lured
into the origins of lucubrations,
the minor sins of firm evaluations;
I've never loved, yet if I hold you close
God will remember us in such a pose.

The Glass Piano

The last stop, the seventeenth century:
such capturements are frozen by the sea
as die hard on the surface of a wave,
dim darkness shepherd of the pilgrim's stave,
starlight in voices, shining to the lee,
pregnant directions of a new country,
split off like atoms shooting aimlessly
in darkest roots of the imagination,
procuring life where there is yet no station ...
How many modes of idiom they see
in spiritual harvests, illumination's bounty,
then spread aloft, complex for eternity,
echoing fixed positions endlessly,
the ladder's rung licked by the adder's tongue ...

The smaller ego is so infinite,
nor words nor gesture shall attach to it,
nor interlocking hands shall bolster it
to heaven, nor shall silence measure it.

Shall persons and shall places shower down
upon the consciousness, capture the town
as it shall be for all eternity,
nor silence measure the entire city.

It is so soft and ticklish at the center,
that born to be beholden to its mentor,
the loving god, all beauty shall prevent her
from falling through the earth that time has lent her.

That living afterwards in perfect form
shall break the flood and smash the wrecking storm.

The Glass Piano

We sit in Central Park, the awful dark
lit up like years by the successive lights ...
I weep, as darkness drowns the sea of nights
in which death swims like a percussive shark ...
Your voice is close to me, as close as Mars
or Venus penetrating through the cars,
ongoing traffic of the crushing stars ...
and empties out diffusive with the bars ...
I seize and clutch your words close to my heart,
who never had been promised a new start ...
and sink into despair, now all my care
is nothing, having no one left to share
the well kept treasures that the night controls,
where all is silence, but the great bell tolls ...

Ben Mazer

Night. We stand beneath a thousand stars,
watching the chariots of the Hamilcars …
the scorpion, the dipper, the big hammer …
tall, earthbound, focused in the heavens' camera …
The island protects us, who live shorter lives,
because the darkness folds like an old movie
around our story which the cosmos gyves,
rippling the curtains, the matchbox of what is to be …
There! There is the place we stood and looked
into each other's eyes; now my resolve is spooked …
I cannot find you, circling in the dark
where all is lost; this voicelessness is stark …
and cannot bring you to my closer knowledge
among the withered leaves and broken foliage.

The Glass Piano

Home was the place I knew night after night,
but I am blind, and all is out of sight ...
I do not recognize my earthly friends,
am intimate now only with what ends ...
The place I stood, the window where I looked
sometimes across the street or through the trees,
in memory is mangled and is crooked,
all's dead beneath the moon's slow-blowing breeze ...
carrying no promises of spring
this year, this year is not a thing ...
No steady mantle I shall lean against
where in my knowledge, everything I sensed ...
but folding myself up inside a star
look inwards for some sign that you still are.

Ben Mazer

And now each place I walk like one who's dead,
surveying the scene where this or that took place,
this ghost beside me, this familiar head,
will bob awhile, then vanish without a trace.
And I am not the things I thought I was,
because the one who held me in esteem
has taken away effect, removing cause,
till all is vanished, someone else's dream.
There is no labyrinth can take me back
to magnetisms that had held in place
the centered world of all that I now lack,
who long once more to look upon her face.
And I am cast in dark eternally,
and live, but shall no longer live to see.

UNE CHIENNE MASONIQUE DANS LA GRANDE LAVATOIRE OCEANOGRAPHIQUE

I

Orthopedic skulls
align the firmament
where stripped of their Catullus
each closed apartment
exchanges moods for time,
the individual sublime,
and heeds no call to duty
beyond rescension's beauty.
Accommodations high
beneath a battered sky
alight with floodlit filth
partake of stellar stealth
and freeze no Hermides
to silences that please
the mother Pere Couchon
but steadily roll on
to thrust accordions
of tridents into dawns,
covert from prying eyes,
the little soul that dies.
Sense cannot regulate
the Platt or river Plate,
industrious and dim,
perched on the edgemost rim
of pleas to abrogate
the pity of sister Kate.
Why should they so abscond,
as if their progress were

replete of all the monde,
all others to aver?
Consigned each to their time,
the annals strict compile
the manner of the house,
the excellence of rhyme
each sequel may defile
according to his mouse,
supportive of the pile
of repetitious crime,
then folded into dawn
awake death to move on.

II

    For Philip Horton

My capital is cultural capital.
But we were young then. The sausages
were plump, and the balconies ripe.
Pressed into service, the elevators
took us to silences without appeal;
you loved one first, then the other.
Tributes to Charleville and Douai
pall on the cheap and bitter tongues
of another generation, west to east.
The wind has abscond with picnics.
I look into the pelted sky
and wonder if we did arrive,
or if the march, the liberated city,
sank seven wonders in its pity.

I have no need to hear from friends.
These ends, too meagre to recall,
revive an aolanthus desperate for the spring
to release joy in the defended city.
Climb into bed, and feel the cold hands fall
to sleep a negro witch burns, steady call
and trumpet of headlights glimmering on the wall.
Until winter I shall have no need to wake,
but hibernate, these letters to partake
of frozen sands, sands frozen, done with switching
the kings of France; monsieur, je desole.

III

My war wounds are a solace to me now.
May turns the fleur-de-lis, a change of valise
that comes to Paris in the spring. I am
the diplomat my fathers were before me.
I carry no fake Bottom in my trousers,
but by degrees stare down the eyes of mausers
trained on the moon, the eyes of pyramids.
The firefly in August turns and flits,
the bowser sits, an aged woman shits
into her coffee. I eat my toffee
and read La Monde. I can't recall how fond
I may have been in youth. I am no hero.
I am still betting
that time will show me in my proper setting,
long past these fevers, and these bouts of gout,
that turn me inwards, when my secret's out.

Ben Mazer

Paris Feb. 28–March 2, 2014

The Glass Piano

The clouds are gathered,
armour in the hall,
the orb of privacy, without the thrall,
meneure de press d'afrique not duly bothered.
The plain of paper, skyline au graphique,
to stern of tramlines, crosshairs ariel;
lasting to night to nominate physique,
rain tightly on the town on thunder fell.
Coordinates in the outlying towns
perpetuated nothing but the sounds
of being, brick and solid, on the crowns
of German metaphysics by the pounds.
My friend resorted to photography;
I graced the garlands of the foretold sea.

Ben Mazer

MISSING PERSONS

What is the point of life,
to those who must put it away?
Years of having a wife,
now each one alone today.
The evenings, the dresses, the words,
conspiratorial smiles,
hearts leaping with joy, flown like birds,
all stuff to be put in the files.
And now ever not to know
the little things that you do,
what heart keeps, the places you go,
missing persons the heart will rue.
Where does it go to, and why,
who knew each other for years,
eyes blind as the terrible sky,
too empty to shed any tears.

Spring Frost

Occasionally when fixed with the purposed
alienation, deviled to the twix
and twin of aviation's aerial
serial: recondite prostration, if you will;
I cannot flap nor flip the concentrates
of abnegation which can't abnegate
but sit here ever softly in the silent
silky greenyear of your coming, by the gate;
come then, be often frosted, nor kin to claim
that evermore the thunderhead has blasted
sin of your crime, or rent me evermore!
I am the spirit of the ghost I wasted;
nor ever, past the wasted, be the same,
past win or winter, dust of the unfrosted.

Ben Mazer

Gradually the house across the way
grew dimmer and brighter, appreciating the stars,
as languidly dropped the words they would have it say,
long in the lucubrations of new lovers,
who sat outside, all hours of the night,
to watch the seasons pass and sense the feelings
of being, divinity untangled from the light
squeezed by the tabula rasa of its ceilings.
Gradually, grown troubled and vexed by poison,
that could not go unnoticed or unencountered,
the fiend undid the gossamer thread of reason,
and the whole season panicked as it floundered.
Desperate with disappointment she duly countered,
breaking her pact with the sun, and moon, and stars.
Tried without sentence, the heavenly funeral biers
shed disapproval crashing where they sauntered.
Now she goes, alone with her cats and fancies.
Her final word has dealt them a fatal blow.
No more of dances, dresses, or of chances.
And God has folded up to see them go.
Then as he changed, for each was forlorn and broken,
he marvelled at the fierceness of her reply,
that she should truly wish to let them die,
saving no shred or scrap of any token,
and their flush season never more go spoken.
The school yard and the flowers and the grasses,
averted their eyes to prospect such cold shrinkage,
now never more each stranger here who passes,
will ponder the eternities of perfect linkage.
To see her face cracked out with frantic horror,

you would be broken too at calm so crippled,
to know there isn't any more tomorrow,
just two cats, sullen and indifferently nippled.
Yet there they lie, prostrate, without recourses,
ploughing the winds of empty solitudes,
not knowing to what degree to feel remorses,
or savour the absence of their finer moods.
No more the bagpipes breathing through the city,
the peopled monuments now all unclaimed
by joyous chatter, eaten up by pity,
no more the great love which was duly famed.
She, one supposes, now has been retired
to simple acts, to duties and to sleep,
while his lot is incognizably mired
in the immense unanswerable deep.

She looks up at the tops of buildings,
the public square. He is not coming.
Everything the same, as it must be.
It lasts a long while, this sameness,
without change, his absence
the same as if he were here.
But he is not coming.
The tops of the churches are so huge,
their stone weight crushes the silence,
and they are interesting.
They persist, persist, but he comes not.
The huge weight of her hands like brick

close her eyes in a sky like tears,
empty and never changing.
But he whose laughter moves the stars,
who made merry with the rings of flowers,
of which she was one, does not come.
The icy words, sealed like a grave,
have put him away forever,
and he cannot come now.

He is here,
oh feel that he is here,
in the stones, in the clouds, in the tears,
washing away the last of last days,
and though she wander forever, forever lost,
he is always here.
But for his part he does not come,
and she must terribly excuse herself
to him, and he must
terribly excuse himself to her,
but he cannot. She must go alone,
nowhere, from stone to weighty stone,
from cat laughter to animal rain of sky,
all ruined now, apart until each die.

The Place

That was the place where once they stood,
incognizant of things done well,
of things that come to any good,
immune to heaven and to hell.
How well they knew each breeze of it,
each leaf, each rock, each branch, each crack
that future generations lack,
nor know that they were part of it.
And yet the summer nights would drop
eternal manna on their heads
just fifty yards from where their beds
held them who came to a full stop.
And yet the long spring afternoons
had stirred with hopes of private things,
that even the poet never sings,
till love itself had come to ruins.

Ben Mazer

Winnie's Tower

Autumn afternoons, between the hours
that time is strictly helpless to impose,
young Winnie takes me up into his towers,
and what is far becomes exceeding close.
The wind's indifference rustles leaves of gold,
and dust puts a pale film upon the air,
Winnie says we're young when we are old,
sensing the ones who were before us there.
Ah, in childhood only the wind troubles desire
on days like these, when all comes to a stop,
but Winnie says that we shall never tire,
dreaming of other lives from his tower top.
Old ivy climbs the tower till it reaches
our revery in which the world seems bare
of all the insignificant, dormant breaches
that intimate to subtle hearts their care.
And though I linger, not ready to go home,
the ghosts of my own former lives will come,
waiting for night, and the full moon to rise,
for we have made such reservations with the skies.

The Glass Piano

Graves and waves are signified by rows,
as is the precedence in church of people,
while there is painted grammar in the rose,
that's juxtaposed against the taming steeple;
one has the cosmos for pulsating rays,
makes chords for sequences by being triple,
that rise up through the hours of our days,
whose distant visages let out a ripple;
the other's pains painted with elaborate stipple,
both finite and elect, and giving pause
to dignity and cause among the living,
who of its grammar make an unforgiving,
a word like weynted, weighted with its flaws,
and draws a circle round the wanted nipple.

Ben Mazer

Brown Hours

To start, a stained glass window holds the time
as centric as a compass point, sublime,
supreme the den of unified religion
holds fluttering still and silence phrygian;
the public emanates from private order.
Brown rituals of inward contemplation
lend service to the optimal equation,
and beauty is as much as we have thought her.
[The man who's civilized must have a daughter.]
The tomes accumulate their docent zeal
for architecture, public works, the real
that passes just outside the private railing.
The unities accept each minor failing
as works of God. The scheme of inner thought
publicly realized, but in private bought.

Supreme the snows make compacts of our youth,
in worlds of gothic walls and stained glass mansions,
both shielding and initiating truth,
the embryo of civilized expansions.
The silver skate, a focus for the foot,
as well as for the rich, obedient daughter,
rings bells for triumph posited at root,
despite the winter's snow blown spray of laughter.
How then the father walks the imminent bride
in moonlight, with the other guests inside,
shall give kind warning of such obligations
as money lends to higher social stations,
spreading old news of fabled Indian chiefs
whose prodigalities bred unkind griefs.

Shing-tu would wander daily to the wharves;
I watched her heading down the morning hill;
the new spring breeze would blow her sun bright scarves;
I see her bobbing downwards towards them still:
the workers on the docks who sold her wares
and told her at what time the ships came through
and where they thought the ships were heading to;
there wasn't that much left for me to do
but ascertain we weren't attracting stares
though she was from that province through and through
and often helped the general up his stairs
while I would write my letters home to you
and wondering at the world I'd ventured to
would lie awake and tell Shing-tu my cares.

The Glass Piano

The general had his coffee on the terrace,
black in china, and a dish of prunes;
he made his calls, and answered morning queries,
and scrawled out indecipherable runes
upon the margins of a newspaper;
I watched the rare birds in his arbor stir;
at nine-fifteen the gardener came in,
and watered roses, then threw in a bin
some twigs and hedges, preparing for the judge's
wheezing entrance on a pair of crutches,
the wind whipped wilder through the new spring trees,
upon a westerly and colder breeze;
serenity had shook me to the core
until his daughter came out through the door.

Ben Mazer

I aspired to be mad like him,
to purse my lips, and rearrange my face
according to some old Italian whim,
and write the history of the Jewish race;
to scare the girls, and sit beside the pool,
on brilliant days some artist colored in,
the master of the compass and the rule,
the pure interpreter of Beethoven;
to snuffle when I chortled, and to spit
upon the church that occupied the corner,
all day in the tremendous garden sit,
to normal obsequies a learned foreigner,
a critic of the local diocese;
espouse the Greek roots of the harmonies;
whose madness seemed like an aesthetic glory,
when I was young, obtuse to the real story.

The Glass Piano

He sauntered briskly on the tennis court,
and stunned the matrons with his supple play,
to whom he proffered all his coy asides,
to stimulate each calyx as he may;
his need was great, though he had well concealed
the origins of all his worldly prowess,
the requisite of his eccentric field
attendance to the summer's bridal showers;
he noted how his daughter, fully grown,
had taken after his peculiar ways,
who made a little fortune of her own,
observing that his method always pays,
his plan to move them to the countryside,
where now the whole expanded clan abide.

Ben Mazer

The Glass Piano

Unfamiliar and incognizant
flat shadows dense oppose expanding time
light scurries there, essence prismatic blent,—
myriad and marmoreal paradigm …
come into focus, and demanding light!
night's clockless teleology of sight
assumes no history, but of wall's stoppage
and window's leakage flowers that are savage
ravage and rack and blight
some lost pearl harbour in the dead of night.
The bombs explode! Just so the glass piano,
which lies so still and patient in the hall,
the predicate of morning—bright Diana! —
lends harmonies to evocate the all.
Leaves flutter—why should they not?—reclaiming space
that scenes are cast in—who could not remember
the absolute interment of motion in place
where heart abided in some lost September?
The crowded episodes dry thunder havocs,
light dimming until old memories are unblind
with ritual escapades, exodus stratospherics,
redeem all distance, portents of the mind.
The hours they live in, empty shells, adornments
of simple wishes, mornings of coffee with friends,
project in violet visages their torrents
of supple lucidity where mind unbends.
They travel far—were distance not an illusion —
only to return, wearier, wiser,
a momentary stay against confusion,
heaped in vast relics absence solidifies there.

The Glass Piano

How can they be upheaved?—the droll bell drones
them whole again, lacking space to confine them,
as if some Europe sauntered to their homes
to rise again, to which the dead shall bind them.
The mind shall settle thus, in slim beliefs
exonerated by its supplication
to static roots, the true note of creation
falling blankly as spent and fluttering leaves.

Alone, who loved her, held in high esteem,
his only solace. Now she goes undone,
unspoken and unheard, and quite alone.
Their highest truth no longer can be seen,
but twists the threads of gossamer that run
through the long night, like someone else's dream,
unanswered and alone, lost what was won,
because misunderstanding has turned mean.
The life they had, perfection's pinnacle,
has turned cold and dry, mechanical,
the soul is dead, and wit no longer keen,
to have fallen thus, to sink so far below
existence as to die without an echo,
and no recourse, and nothing to be done.

A New-Fangled Prodigal

To dream a world on a hunk of shade,
throw back the schedule of the maid,
and meditate in bedsheets, dim
where the morning light is slim,
studying objects that recall
the continents to a hand held ball,
tracing out rivers with calipers,
shadows in brambles the spider endures,
contemplate a bit of repartee
one brought back home from foreign stay,
and leave the rose-scented soap untouched,
receiving callers, breathless and flushed,
is only to follow the organized plan
of the modern, ecclesiastic man,
forwarding goodness by intuition,
measurement, calculus, and division,
exercising divine revision
with a maximum of precision.
Why then does this one find no words
to trace the motion of the birds,
unsettling up from the garden rose,
sipping and sampling the gardener's hose,
and what is it, finally, that this one knows?
Only the music that is exquisite,
as ladies come calling on Sunday visit,
best in their finery like latest news,
veritable aviaries of Paris views,
shaded in quarantine, oblong, obscure,
but for all that he lacks, spanking bright demure.
It rises to tree tops and looks over steeples,

and though misanthropic of many peoples,
its harmonic strains cut with tenderness through
the shroud of his sick bed and his universe too.

The Glass Piano

Grandma Florence went riding over the hills,
past the author's house, past the place with the lemon pies,
which we would return to on the way back she said,
to where the country is free and up ahead
New England apple orchards gleam and shine
in the Connecticut Valley. Thirty or forty years
they took this route, when there was nothing there,
to see old friends, extended family,
purveyors of business, business of all kinds,
stern advocates of schools improving minds;
now Grandma Florence beats down the hills alone,
knowing full well how this one up and died,
how that one lost a fortune or a wife,
how these were successful, did everything almost right;
Grandma Florence preserved a word or two
for principles she had picked up along the way,
but what they were, no one could get her to say;
only she turned to me sometimes—with a hiss like a curse—
and uttered a line or two of good English verse.

Ben Mazer

I
The molar ankle of the house's disconnect
is lapt in the exhaustion of the sea.
Or will it rise, a blackbird on a wire,
to chiaroscuros the invidious see,
and take some other form, blent with eternity
to empty words of all experience
where this one speaks to that one to commence …
Shall they arrive, where? Rift, parti-colored birds
that stay excursus to one hum-drum beat
of lynx-strewn jungle, from the ashes rise
to glimmer on the subway past your eyes
in arbitrary cities stone-hewn gods
demarcate, elevating higher than
co-ordinates opposed to gravity …
to know one name, and always knowing thus,
slip out of harness, had there been no Rome …
but stricter deserts, slim conglomerates
of wastage and relief, words fully blown
to madness where the flowers blossom grief
and love the singing wire of a stone …

II
Rows and rows of trees bound northward still …
release the shadows where the acorns fall
or rise with summer, steadier to be full …
eclipsing shadows, raking down the sky
where eyelash travels, houses the blind can see …
their molar windows iridescent plates,

shale's cobalt stoppage ... stacked piles of croppage prim,
directions of desire ...
names bubbling to the mind until they brim,
silencing the tongue ... reap steady with arms full
magnificence that seethes a vacancy,
the questing wills press on ... empty of memory torn
from steadier altars rising to be born ...
then closing latches, accepting obscurity.

III

Alert to traces, in the transept's pouch,
the earthen lead-wear of the stippled mouth
conveys the rumbling of explosive wings
in noon's dim cellar, musty beyond recall ...
words of the dead, they hammer and they swing
to regent arteries of avenues
transactions throttle ... tall to limestone rims
the governor mottled, knowing of profit's eyes ...
then shrink into obscure and byzantine
rescensions of proud privacy ... they ball
and jar the city's sceptre, palaces that crawl
to heaven, the dead blasting of the bells,
corporeal of magnate compound hells ...
All this on Kingston Avenue I've seen.

IV

Then fluming there, industrial gardens bloom
to perfect peace, their harmonies forswear
the carriage of the voice past pale facades

of wicker summer, latticed underlings
that splay the earthworm, pack light in a jar
where one may supervise a cup of tea
and know strange idioms of a caller's mind
to scramble arbours, portents invisibly
forceful of dramas where the heroes fail
to grasp expedient onslaughts of hail ...
They draw within ... slim intimacies that bind
all columns horizontal, vertically ...
the individual progress of the blind,
look up surprised, the beloved guest to see ...

V

Variably the entrances to summer
protect the profligate, convert the wealthy,
past their observances, to some state beyond ...
the mill-house or the minnow-dappled pond
where the splatched bark of dusty men is healthy ...
then into the dark woods —
compelling birth demarcates frigid air —
the welkin saddled, brush of undertow
darker than townhouses where they go ...
etched walls of silver principles confess
to other stationaries, pals for life ...
hoping to return, no dagger, and unbruised,
been to the center, back to take a wife.

VI

Jarred to some stop, that some can understand,

newspaper pearl, the local act of speech
all of defiance in immediate reach
blurs the sub-ice way, all falls to a lurch ...
No need, familiar, to lie. Stacked to the horizons of the sky
this people's letter, embedded now in brick
or shadow, to the watch-perch of the widow.
What these newspapers print don't duly die ...
So, blown on your scarf in Vermont creams
that shame ship launchings, and retract a mayor,
the fool of civilization is self launched;
and one can say that you were duly there.

Ben Mazer

DOUBLE PLOT

Captured by the immediacy of time,
where older Boston is residual
on long drives home, colored electric lights
plying the winding, rising, falling night's
echoes of suppositions, piercing the dark,
dim embers of the sleeping go unstirred,
yet live in motion strangling the veins …
their spirits like double vision at the panes
of glass that peruse each familiar, frozen sight,
the mall lot with its fantastic electric light …
as if some memory, unconscious, might
revive a principle that chokes the soul,
the chattering utterance of an intuition …
the closed grand Petersburg rows of Beacon Hill
hidden among the throngs of shadowing flowers,
stasis in motion that animates the hours …
elect some conversation, long disposed,
to mythic states, life chapters that have closed …
were battered by some strange, insistent ghost
demanding satisfaction, the holy host
of life as spirit, even when unlived …
How many nights the darkness has forgiven
the never enacted, and the life unshriven …
then rising to life in the heart's throbbing ghost,
recalled the archetypal situation,
as if to briefly hold reality,
and not some long world's arbitrary city,
no more unreal than arbitrary Rome,
as if it were the veins' own ghostly home,
closed in the silence of the car's museum,

reflective lights will scatter chaotically
in sleeping rhythms, sensible to the nerves
that swing legato round the turnpike's curves ...
and resurrect, as if to make a man,
the birth of consciousness where time began ...
some piercing, primal, modern observation
of what we are, disturbing the sensation ...
some absence tearing the heart with its vacation ...

Ben Mazer

High alcoves, orange walls rising to the night
that twists and turns beyond the high orange light,
friends share one corner of eternity,
the felt and cut-out absent property
of consciousness alone with memory
and supposition, what one cannot see
whorled in the nerves' conjecture, where the world,
reduced to stasis, intimation curled
around the ceiling or some dim high tree,
explodes with language, parrying the mind's
rudderless unanchored rootless root
of sheer existence, chattering to boot
some strong familiar echoings that climb
up to the skylight, tokens of their time …

Shakespearean, the formulations blur
and stir the fresh dew on the hoods of cars,
and settle sleepers, invisible, demure
where streetlights scamper underneath the stars
at each dull intersection, duly veined
with fragments of Elizabethan, stained …
The high gods of palatial homes confer
a counterpoint in group experience
upon the eager, willing, and the dense
riled up dramatic children to commence
ejaculations rituals aver …
but these must falter in midnight's appearance,
and climb back into principles to hide,
torn from all property and unallied …

Yet shall draw unity still to exclaim
the madrigality the conscious claim ...

Anent no world, blasted in dark storm
to keep the bedclothes of the sleeping warm ...

[Unconsciously they wait for God to cure
existence of history and make them pure ...]

Ben Mazer

To look at them, who moved so easily
between the garden or the railway station,
who sat for hours where the boats came in,
with little movements fused in unity,
as if each were a breeze jostling the other,
drinking their coffee, talking of next to nothing,
could one perceive what brought these two together,
firm in their bond through any kind of weather?
Now that their endless conversation's done,
the morning cigarettes, and seaside sun,
the fairs, the city days, the nights alone,
who is there to pardon or condone
the reasons such a two should be as one,
or make a world out of the observations
they shared through all their many incarnations,
or break the existence of their summer dinners,
or other such bright realities disperse?
A cat might notice: lace curtained unities
of street and tree, long pregnant nights in winter,
of rainy days through all their perorations;
but what is there left to give the faintest hint
or evidence that these two did exist?
Now they are done, by whom shall they be missed?

Poem

No prose the mystery of summer nights
plummets—but images the darkness skirt
towards light, the blurred and reached for sights
of elemental visages that hurt;—
they hang there, brushed by moonlight, sweeping clouds
that move towards continents vast and unseen:
and gently rustle, nascent, dormant shrouds:
incandescent fragments of what we've been;—
they move the mind, that moves on images,
stuck in the darkness of its slow resolve;
and turn, as moonlight softly turns its pages,
emotions on the crescent rim of love;
then vanish, all their proudness for the ages,
traceless unless star-captured up above.

Ben Mazer

'In curtained images, stung by the asp!'

Tear away, oh tear away the veil
that doth conceal the maker his beloved;
in spangled images, the love you feel
dissolves, immaculate cleft clouds above it;
white summer sweaters tease the mind's desire
for solvent matter, on which it can stake
the meaning, cumbrous, of the fading fire
that blurs like flickering candles, for love's sake;
grown farther distant, out of the palm's reach,
the nimble visages the mind has quested:
shall these, or other fragments, shake the breach
of absolution that desire requested;
or shall they falter, fade into the dim
and calming ruin where true love began.

The Glass Piano

The idle roofs are slags and crags
of chunks against a mildewed sky;
the weight of human history sags,
and rain ensnares eternity.

The mind absorbs the present's waste,
and stumbles forth with humble haste;
no human heart for miles around
is gleaned or makes the slightest sound.

The night comes on. Enveloping rain
ameliorates the glow of pain,
that grows, although its face is numb,
and all its origins are dumb.

Turn in the car lot; spin around;
electric lights without a sound
shed color and a point of view:
man circles, nothing left to do.

Go, make your midnight pilgrimage there:
the empty lot, the empty square,
fall back into some sleeper's dream,
and have no elemental theme.

Ben Mazer

The Styrofoam Clown

It rains. The afternoon for your pains
revises a detective who surmises
the little appointments upon which life sustains
its sense of ease reverting to surprises.
The common wife of public curiosity
anoints the hours, implacable to see
the settled paws on roofs of broken leaves,
the orphan which a prince's drowning leaves.
All fall I sit here writing you this letter,
knowing better [now]
the sorts of things that you would have me say,
things that go neither this way nor that way,
things that mark no day.
Yet, summoned, I will rise to meet the debtor
of what you've left here in my empty arms,
smiles that the sky smiles, smiles without any charms,
and look about for miles, where sundry harms
can bring no profit to their one begetter.
Accounts of breezes, verges of dark shading
release such perspicuities from raiding
an assumed memory,
vestigial, compartmental,
in lieu of substances more elemental,
this symphony,
lacking verification
these evening sunsets which are so delicious,
the placard wishes
of a philosopher, a styrofoam clown.
The morning swept up by its evening gown
again comes down

to heave the hours
into recessive, regent pointillisms
of nascent flowers;
thus I have set the table for my schisms.
Weak then, not knowing what to do by you
I scan the paper for some key announcement
that is as if I thought such things should be,
but lacking strength to make some great pronouncement,
folding the newspaper, accepting by degree
the thousand forms that take this mystery,
relieve myself of thoughts of you and me,
antiphonies of no objectivity,
knowing the burden of philosophy.
Should fold my panoramas in one album,
folded and ribboned, and left to be unopened,
the faintly bright and fragmented amalgam,
not quite sensation, groping every rope end
of what the autumn has brought back to me,
for I have known such full blown prophecy
as sinks each naiad in the surging foam
of unkempt desire, uncertain that any home
will unify or marry all my fire.
This spectacle of which my wishes tire …

Ben Mazer

The Golden Pear

    for Ivan Kustura

Nowhere are shadows swept more tall nor deep
as where in the walkways of the midnight hour
the long low friends move slowly, as if to steep
God's own unconsciousness with inner power,
silently blazoned where their memories keep
cool casements resonant of summer's tower,
talkless where richnesses have yet to weep.
Turn then, and face away; eternity
shall never again make any room for these
poor figures, stuck in their dream of happiness
richer than any kingdom or provinces,
and keep your eyes, though there be nothing left to see.

The Glass Piano

When like a perjured idiot I ran
into the calling of my great despair,
I tried to speak, but could not heed my care,
until in ruin lay all I began
ten thousand nights ago in my great need
beneath the lordly green catalpa tree
that steadied me, whose steady anchor freed
the steady years to my great potency,
the gossamer-threaded scene of ecstasy
where timeless I queried the divinity
as to the substance of what I must be,
and worked the anvil of my force and creed;
thus dying thus, I saw before me fold
my charge, so absolute, I had been told.

Ben Mazer

To go back now, is to relinquish trust
in the compelling ocean of existence,
sweeping over memory, to realign
a thousand swift, ethereal coordinates,
no longer bone as tree, surrounding flowers,
but tempting shades, to lead one away,
intoning prayer, no body in the grave
to expand in sense to what we were,
yet the hard inversion of satiable death,
compels me to try to enter forbidden spheres,
convert to pearls my necklaces of tears,
if only to appease the gods' immense
and recondite refusals on their terms,
challenging life to rise to its opaque
and reverent madness, enter the baroque
false stations that signify another world;
so I begin, for eternal beauty's sake
to knock on skeletons to let me in,
drowning in seas of grass, illimitable
and blue, and dazzling comprehension
to find the flower of my former state,
some idle armchair where I sat to prate
upon a garden's boundaries I knew,
the concentration of a china cup
hard in the hand, and central to the order
of a conversation's inherent border,
illuminable, and swift in rural myth
to reach the edges of substantiation;
o I have known fulfillment and elation!
at what you are, significant in death,

The Glass Piano

the heaping of treasure in a distant star
that smooths the evening, sitting where we still are,
symphonic exonerations of which I sing,
the hard transactions nimble beyond all sting,
in permanence beyond extinguishing,
the steadfast template of the Hamilcars,
wayward in desire. Afflicted fires.

Ben Mazer

TREES

Were trees always what they seem to be?
They were not. I built this tree for thee.
Thick with all kinds of years I can't remember
they hang above my head in climbing tiers
of branches, many levels of thick leaves
in nights of silence that go on forever.
How can I recognize what they say or mean
when nothing is the same? Are they the same?
I think that I am blind and have no thoughts.
All the is's, was's now are nots.
What is not? The tree which over me
put my head asleep so I can't see.

The Glass Piano

The visible soda shop, arresting form,
De Rerum Natura, where the sun will warm
flounces of skirts, Catullus well denied
where motion asserts its spirit, yet implied
in contemplation of fave movie stars,
or charming boys who've purchased their first cars:
what scene projected on to Plato's cave
can give full body to the love they crave?
They sip their drinks, in modern effigy
of all the general thrust of history,
and simplify themselves by looking good,
and by behaving as they're told they should.
What pictures though go roaming through the brain!—
that makes its own distinctions, personal
and mythic as the spirits that attain
distinctive wardrobes, plaid wool for the fall.

Ben Mazer

I moved through my huge family's world,
of aunts and grandmothers who smoked,
beyond stacked floors of my age hurled
to darkness, while the whole clan joked.
These scenes I entered somewhat late,
were volumes of strange histories,
no wealth of stories satiate
my passion for the unities.
As such a ghost, I walked among
the remnants of a time half gone,
aware the timing was all wrong
to long for what I might have known.
Instead, a prince in their estate,
I took comparisons to rate
the world I knew with what had been,
all hints of things I had not seen;
illustrious in my fresh art
of knowing worlds a world apart,
I drew conclusions from the whole,
substantiations of the soul.

The Glass Piano

I saw her once, I don't know where I was
or whether I dreamed, but she was so familiar
it was as if in life she spoke to me:

"You cured my life, and made me well again,
but after time I knew that I must leave you,
not because you lacked any success,
or qualities that make a woman love a man,
but because you strayed from me, because
something went wrong somewhere in your heart,
so when I spoke to you it was not you,
but someone in a fever of distraction
whose focus was entirely elsewhere,
and fearing for the oncoming of age,
I knew that I must act to save myself ...

"It was the hardest thing I ever did
to let you go, to let go my own heart,
reasoning to save us both our happiness,
to sacrifice—as was my character—
myself to the liberty you seemed to need ..."

Then I, as tears began to swell my eyes:
"If I had known, if I had woken up
from the great dream that crushed me in its vice,
I would have poured my heart out through my eyes
to ask forgiveness, and return to you ...
No matter what I did, my own heart knew
all truth and beauty, all I knew of love,
had emanated from the source of you,

who was too lucky with his lot in life ...
When God decreed that you should be my wife
I stumbled and I fell, not looking back
even to notice what I myself had done,
who wept more water than the seven seas
when you had left me speechless and alone ..."

The restaurants were peopled once again,
as they had been in life; there was still time
for conversation and the little things
that seem so real they fill us with belief ...

Then it was she did a peculiar thing:
she handed me a single tiny pearl,
and kissing me on the forehead like a child,
she spoke as if to speak for one last time:
"Take this, in time which you may recognize
is crowded inside, like angels on a pin,
with all the things we said, and all we were,
so tightly bound it never can unwind ...
This relic, keep forever close to you,
that nothing is undone, and what we were
shall keep you whole for all eternity ..."

She turned, though I expected to hear more,
some sign of life that could bring back the past,
and seemed entirely preoccupied
with something very distant that she saw ...
Then I turned too, and clutching my small pearl,
looking to see what it was she saw,
but there was nothing there ... Then she was gone ...

I turned in long strides towards oblivion ...
The night came on, and memory was extinguished ...

Ben Mazer

The sea is no longer the sea,
the sands are no longer the sands,
since you have departed from me,
and left my memories melting in my hands.
I gaze far into the sky above the sea,
looking for you in the distance, but all I see
is a childhood of blue, and the flags of England and France
waving across the ocean invisibly.
The clouds have been true to me,
and follow me out of the past,
from when we're together at last,
as far as the eyes can see.
From weddings to which we have been,
of relatives who have died,
remembering how we sighed,
on walks that won't come again.
Lucretius said the clouds
form into what has been,
implying history sucks,
and lovers can never win.
Catullus wept his tears
in fragments on the page,
but you were far more sage,
so far beyond all years.
The myrtle and the woodbine
take forever to combine,
is this how it is with us,
rendezvous terminous?
All that we've been before,
somehow got stuck in the door,

and I am not as I was,
but, absent, remain with us.
Imagine if we had once known,
the nothing to which things have come,
had accounted the total sum,
of all that we had been shown.
Each day that we thought was forever
well hid the fact we would sever,
and everything given the lie
was lived only that it should die.
All the positions we took,
the positions and the decisions,
are worth an eternal look,
should all go into the book
of earth without any revisions.
The libraries slept that we sauntered past,
as we walked into town,
nothing holds any more interest
now that we are shut down.
But most what I miss is the kiss
on that wild night in the gazebo,
when we made our eternal vow,
before things had come to this.
And though the brilliant water, white and black,
at sundown burns in answer to the sun,
depthless until eternity is done,
I must face it, I am all alone,
there is no way to push the long tide back.

Ben Mazer

*

Too much loss, free-manic takes the wheel.
No point in telling anyone how I feel.
Six years gone, then back to Davis Square one.
I comb the midnight silence of Orchard Street.
I move a block, and then another block.
Over in Cambridge, the cat sits by the window
and thinks of me. How excited he would be
to see me emerge from darkness, returning warrior.
How could I whisper to him and not wake you?
The summer conceals the snow of my first poem,
the winter of revelations. The silent hours,
marred only by rustling leaves and passing cars,
remember my steadfast loyalty to you,
something I never explained to anyone.

*

Drunk Picasso-white distorted adobe,
unfindable side street of another year,
your Mexican blanket patterns of the mind
sank dizzy in the undertow of fatigue,
coupling desire with visual satisfaction,
giving new lease to myths of strawberries,
old bright orchards of the secret caravan
I dangled my feet by, in the mirroring reeds.
The dusty volumes emptied of passing years
complete my education. Lost I find
the semblance of a primitive state of mind,
houses oblong, round, triangular,

a side street leading back to Babylon,
the painter's canvas a yell to no one's window.

*

The savage stillness of Heraclitus streams
down Claremont streets at midnight … Nothing sleeps
but people, cadavers of the daylight hours.
We're free! The urge to procreate all mischief
watches each house's personality
of brick, of wood, of lawn, of gossamer
windows. Only the darkness sees
the wavering shadows of leaves in reverse.
We carry our shoes, conversing to rehearse
the idle memorials of a world gone wrong,
the tireless babble of Diana streams,
lofty for Mexico, a quick escape;
the zipcar rushes past metallic lights,
to flowering rooftops segmenting the night.

*

The ten yard pass, brick ivy-covered brick
that rots in sleep, while eighty years ago
is memory retrieved, the ribboned love letters
locked in a drawer with stacks of TV Guides;
the twenties lie alone and sick in beds,
but turn the key in the empathic head,
just short of rain. The rise of corner lines
amplify the distance from our minds,
of old and modern pioneering dreams.
Man stands alone, with no one to confide
his ecstasies, his broken down desires.

Ben Mazer

Sheer nothingness shuttles along the hours,
and by your strange and pertinent request,
revive the timeless patterns of the flowers.

The Glass Piano

I tried to find you in that surging mob
of people fleeing deasil-widdershins,
but swift eternity would never stop,
nor would god pardon any for his sins ...
All grew into a fervoured disrepair
of people tumbling every sort of way,
I searched the fog but couldn't see you there,
my lips were mumbling things I had to say ...
Was then I realized where I might have been,
struck by a ghost's familiarity,
the rags and market lanes of countless men
and women stretching far as I could see ...
All I'd forgotten came back in a flash,
strange places I had visited on earth,
known faces as I made my breathless dash,
imagination that preceded birth ...
I saw the lanterned gardens of old love,
of places I had never even been,
all indistinct as memory's treasure trove
of what the heart keeps silently within ...
Was then I realized I was truly lost,
in scenes without beginning, without end,
and reckoned the immensity of cost,
of loving you, of having had a friend ...

Ben Mazer

Thirties Poem

To love you I have to carry a spear in my hand,
roast a pig and a pineapple on a spit,
go diving for pearls, telegraph by wireless
the coast guard and mainland that we aren't coming home.
Naked we channel the loop of a waterfall,
breathless and coming up drenched and shaking our heads,
counting the stars and the lights of the ships at sea,
one utterance, of scurrying officers monotony.
How many flights like this one has modern man
archetypally repeated in Tangiers or Turkestan,
one voice in the wilderness, swimming and making a plan,
waking in morning to pearls in a coffee can.

Berryman at Columbia

They always give you something at the movies,
Harlem flashing like ships colliding at sea,
the fireball that came in and goes out with me,
the rim of a cumulative entelechy.
Settling in fog, two eyes that pierce the mist
while New York sleeps, the Pleiades have hissed
their asp-like horrors in my deafened ear,
stately memorials of the incipient year.
The bells, I say, the bells break down their tower
and swing to meet the light of speed this hour,
when all in darkness tiptoes like a ghost
upon the stairway of the holy host,
and smiles on infant Jesus in his bed,
while migraines block out all the words we said.

Ben Mazer

'Twas then I knew the meaning of the sea,
how it had washed men's souls of memory,
and gathered every weather to its cup,
that only God could ever drink it up,
as various as rainstorms that deride
the known world in the torrents of their tide.
The subway lurched, the strangers were all ghosts
who sullen in their chatter and their boasts,
displacing time, compiled a monstrous city
too vast for anonymity or pity
to drink them up. I started to go home.
My heart was beating like a metronome.
Then we came up, the city came in view,
a gargoyle's eyes the ships were passing through.

Greens dark and light of evergreen and fir
are permeated by the campus light
squinty as pepsodent, spectral as northern light
that stirs the goose, and unfurls the swan,
narcissus of the hours before the dawn
where deer walk by unnoticed and are gone.
My mind's not right. Like founts of Fontainbleu
across the street the power station lawn
feeds memories of so much that is gone,
without a center to hold them together.
A lonely bench somewhere in Central Park,
the afghan silence of another life.
Coffee in morning in the stately garden
of my first marriage. Nothing holds together.
But now I am happy again anew,
loving a girl from Sodus, Fontainbleu.
She is asleep. I try my memories on,
splinters and fragments like the splitting light
piercing the firs and the perennials,
perennials of absence in the heart,
of how I started pristine at the start.
The blurry jigsaw puzzle of the night
has depths that ooze the kodak of the light.

Ben Mazer

Word

As O's make circles of the rain,
mindful of the empyrean,
so words are sentences that close,
subtractions from what the world knows.

Gesture

The lights came on. The theatre
was circled in a frame of rain.
The wind beat like another world
against the roof and on the eaves.
A figure dressed in hat and cane
in motions challenging duration
like light across the sky was hurled,
announcing his mute peroration.
The audience squirmed. He tumbled, fell;
from footlights rose the flames of hell;
he snagged his cane, and caught it well,
each fixed eye holding him aloft,
until it couldn't stand the strain;
and then the world went dim and soft.

Perhaps some one of you has lost a friend,
a dozen summers, love that knows no end,
a million dinners, afternoons of rain
and cups of tea, immeasurable pain
that slips between the fingers and the thumbs,
then turns to tears as some old memory comes.
Perhaps all gain is a perpetual hurt
that leaves you crying face down in the dirt
at what you've done, destroying what was won
at such great cost, when there is only one
who you no longer tell your troubles to.
The nights are long with so much left to rue,
and lovely breezes slice with such sharp pain,
evoking what will never come again.

Ben Mazer

When memory depletes, a slow peace comes
that has no pact with what you knew before,
the way the winter snow's vast carpet drums
its brilliant shadows on the wall and door,
stifling sleep, stirring imagination
to myriad branches of eternity,
the tabula rasa of pristine creation,
with metaphors for metaphors eyes see.
Then we were whole, and welled up in ourselves
the perfect stillness of a pregnant faith,
like clock-wound figures silent on the shelves,
or some revealing antiquated wraith.
Now nothing comes, not even dropping peace
to quell the unrest of life's shortened lease.

The Glass Piano

These highways littered with the oxes skulls,
burning to dreams, the fever of our lord,
hallucinations far from their Catullus,
have put an ague on the fevered word.
Directionless, the fathoming of man,
in all his motions, and his veil of blood,
the wastes of sand extend a caravan,
of pilfered surplices, and prayers of mud.
How shall the numbers of incoming space,
so high they dazzle the eternities,
of locus make such absences a place,
where broken bones can't wash out to the seas,
where, separate as dreams, the human race
takes animals for partial deities.

Ben Mazer

Bix Beiderbecke (1903–1931)

When Bix had reached the end, he was obscure,
and wandered all day in the public park,
whose tone had been so brilliant and so pure,
but in decline had faded in the dark.
He met a girl, who hardly knew that he
had been the king of jazz, the rhythm king
of Whiteman's band, the best band in the country,
now in the rain his leg would ache and sting,
broken by mobsters, but he was demure
and dapper in his proud and run down way.
There wasn't much that they would really say,
and there was nothing left for him to choose;
the nights were painted all in blacks and blues,
and when the end came no one heard the news.

A Pastoral Interjection

This spade, this barrow, and these spade-bright leaves,
that link the morning's breezes with tomorrow,
reflect a Cyclops where great absence sieves
the gardener's joy, and drains it of its sorrow.
Young children play at David and Goliath,
to find them there, where history doth uncover
in the old sense, the chrysalis behemoth
of pristine senses that inspire the lover.
They run and play! No where to run to grieves
the absent wishes that their childhood leaves
to other days; the gardener rocks and sways;
the archer's model follows all their days,
making contiguous borders of green swards,
turning them back to the created words.

Ben Mazer

When we were young, our poetry shot stars
that lit up all the morning's gardens,
the predicates of Tyres and Hamilcars,
but we get older, and true vision hardens.
Then we knew such languid mysteriousness
as met conquistadors, and rested silent
upon the sleeping windows, subtleties of less
than being, incalculably violent!
In rich obscurities of endless treasure
the minutes lapsed, and caved in all the hours,
the roots of our paroxysms of pleasure,
such unknown lives as we could claim were ours!
But now society has racked and bent
all innocence, and poetry is spent.

The Glass Piano

Words are just words
unless their combination
alert the fabric of the senses to
the deeper issues that the spirits rue
in images like carpets of northern snow
blinding out time, and making the old new
so then words are like a snowman talking to
the icy breath of god that skirts the powder
soft and glittering, building by the hour
as blank a sheet as words could hope to meet
to fully know themselves, and knowing you
convey the thing that's only yours to say
at midnight while the others are away
in sleep, the clock ticks, and the snow is deep,
deeper than love letters ribboned in a drawer
of loves that will bother no one any more
and abstract figures, like diagrams on the wall
remind one of all history and its fall
into the present, darkly incandescent
for flowing at the edge, of ever, all—
brilliant and wide-eyed, and possessed of body
the snow itself reflectively as haughty
as full blown words that they are drawn upon,
that flow forth in the immanence of song—
what can they mean, to strangers never seen,
who hear a different morning at the desk
of pencil, telephone, and persian carpet,
out of which the fresh words must invent
the reasons that imagination's sent
to know such ghosts, to welcome stranger hosts

into the private parlour that they vent
to resurrect the fabric, bright and pure,
of such sonatas as they may infer ...
and looking this way, blind and heaven sent,
to know the crux of the familiar scene,
the densest whiteness that has ever been ...
sad shadows fallen on a pallet screen
in interplay, where light must needs be lambent
to splay the chlorophyll of all its glint
and resurrect the fragments like a magnet
to teach the alien stranger how to speak ...
before the heart grows too full and must break
for any ordinary wordless sake,
then end in silence that the makers make
of snow and moon and tree that time must take ...

Holy Sonnet

Heaven take me if my nearer soul
should merge in unity when I am gone,
who were one another's each and other,
inseparable when the earth was on;
fly to my heaven, let me see again
my radiant happiness, my true and one
who made me whole on earth, let what I am
be granted death to suffer only birth;
expede my progress, let me not lag too late
in blindness with which life has blasted me;
no more my mangled and distorted heart
can grope through darkness, hoping to be free;
to know the hours that would sing and prate,
bring you to me, and promise a new start.

Ben Mazer

Skiing After Nazis in Ottawa

People my age look like people who were older.
How many oceans have I swam
solo since the world began?
I lost the world. Now what have I returned to?
Or can I return? The trees are swept away
which filled my nights for an eternity.
An epoch and a generation drowned
in dazzling voyages without a sound.
The moon still shines on strangers in a train
who have appointments with strange private pain.
Gone to the country for their lost adventures,
exonerating time their love indentures.
And how should I look up from all I've lost,
survey and try to estimate the cost
when all is gone? Reporting now to no one,
this strange and fabulous oblivion
has marked my time in notches, buried deep
within the mid-night garden where vines creep
towards a speculative and loaded stillness,
sinking desire. I register my illness,
and summon ghosts' assistance to go on.
I shall sit here serving tea to no one,
and counting all my marvellous ordeals,
long false contrivances time deftly steals,
as if I had some counterpart who feels
the crux of witness backing my appeals.
And can I say that I've been loyal to
the firm example that was set by you?
Shall I put skies on that I might pursue
nazis in Ottawa? This broken train

the sole witness to conflicted pain
that ends my story, and nullifies the glory
of nascent clouds that penetrate the rain,
such as I've know, never to come again?
I have no further use for history,
yet sit here looking out across the lee,
marking the time my eyes have failed to see.
When we two, one another's best,
cast out upon the ocean's brilliant breast
confirming in sensation what is real,
the realized form surpassing the ideal,
eternity stopped to hear the things we say,
and crowded all the hours with verity.
Since you are gone, your splendour no more seen,
and space surrender all that we have been,
no one will question what the living mean,
or spy our figures cast out on the sea.
All is quite dead, there is no evidence
of what so long ago we did commence.
Now no one can reproduce what we have felt,
or can withdraw the blow that death has dealt.

Ben Mazer

The sun was shining, and the yucca-yuk
was pounding shrill indentures in my ear.
My horn-rimmed glasses straddled my thick head,
and shone with my reflection in my beer.
Uncle Ricardo's coat gone from the wall,
they were all in church. Lord Thomas said
the dead would sleep their drinking off in bed.
I cursed myself, and grumbled to my keys,
though you have lost your dress, I still need these.
My wife was panicked that I'd gone too far,
past Scylla and Charybdis in the family car.
I beat my hams, and counted my lost friends;
the woe of madness rarely ever ends.
I slit my bible where the rainbow bends.

The Glass Piano

Our logic will not seem to do
whose lines are broken, wholly round,
sensation's work, the instinct's clue
to loves that fall without a sound,
and cannot tell you where or who
you must petition, pound for pound.
Marie is like the moonlight's streak
that runs across her summer hair,
but one will never hear her speak,
or take her measure, if she's there,
although emotion reach its peak,
eternity bereft and bare.
So we are slender of conceit,
for trampling grounds with muddied feet.

Ben Mazer

I also can recall distinct sensation
on mountaintops, or any place at all
where I have wintered on my school vacation,
in Acapulco, remnants of the fall.
How movie stars would fight the winds to speak,
over the glimmer of their scarves and pearls,
over their margeuritas and their steak,
how in the wind the moonlit clouds would swirl.
But I am closeted with my sensations,
and face the mirror of the inner door,
knowing no way to speak of my elations,
that end in grief. The world will know no more
of kingdoms that withstood my shaking heart,
when time will break this looking-glass apart.

And when I look upon the moon
I sometimes get the vague idea
that it was all a little soon
to dream of love for you and me.
In Peter Pan, you had the part
of Wendy, and it broke my heart
to hear you sing so sweet and high;
I wept to think that you could die.
And though I followed you all fall,
you finally wrote me vicious poems
of cars that plummeted in lakes
because you had removed the brakes.
And that's the way that young love goes:
no talking, and no getting close.

Ben Mazer

And what comes after? Let there be a daughter
to keep your loneliness amid much laughter.
Beyond, I shall not witness from the grave
the world you make, the culture that you save.
I will miss all, long buried in the ground,
when in the world you will still run around,
and reach the peak of your maturity,
the future carry on my legacy,
and all the world resound with your fine words,
amidst new generations of spring birds.
Then I'll die proud, at what you have become,
who of divinity's whole holy sum
shall make the world inspired, who shall come
to fabulous wisdom after I am gone.

The Glass Piano

The car sweeps round the curves and winding lanes
with other cars and whizzing spots of light
past vaguely lit up lawns of waving trees
and houses where half-buried in the night
the educated and intelligent
conduct their normal lives in privacy
while midnight glides around the sleeping city,
awakening pity in the insomniac
who's stupefied and stupored by the still
revolving images the windshield yields
to mark as definite the present time,
then presently the car inclines and climbs
up to a further stillness wider spread
with space and larger houses on a hill
rushed past so fast a horse's skeleton
might pound across an abandoned overpass
to mark the outskirts of the whole wide pool
of citizens who populate the world:
the time is now, and fumbles at its image in the mirror
to see the flesh it touches restlessly
in dumbness knowing life as legendary.

Imagined grandeur covets and conceals
bright lights and silver trays of life's ideals
in Cambridge houses, holding out of reach
such formulations as professors teach,
the private banter, works of art in oil,
to men in alleys, broken in their toil.
And I am passing, with a madman's thoughts,
decisive passing notes through magisterial slots,
imagining the first edition scores
on the piano, bought before the wars,
and flower vases sitting there for years,
and private rooms with laughter and with tears.
And when it rains, then what do they withhold,
the attic lairs unvisited and cold,
that are so full? I stop and lift my eyes
to scan the branches beating on the skies,
and wonder what's inside. Mysterious eaves
are dumb to speak beneath the shaking leaves.
I think, who am I with a heart so black
it aches just to imagine what I lack,
all brightly lit with warmth at Christmas time,
the only formulation of a mime,
without effects or causes, or connections,
to supercede these vacant derelictions.

The Glass Piano

The little girl who stumbles like a hen
is closer to us than the heart of man
She throws her arms and cackles to the sky
then falters by some ivy on a fence
Her concentration is intense
but easily interrupted
to whirl about pristine and uncorrupted
oblivious to the rain
She turns and spins
and stumbles back the other way again
Her back to us
I wonder what she sees shouting to heaven
holding a rag doll like a younger brother
and heedless in some deep way of her mother
I shall not gain such innocence again
but think the world has fallen on its face
to let her down with evil and disgrace

Ben Mazer

The mantel clock
conforms the space
that's motionlessly hurled throughout the world
From underneath some letters
there peeps a sock
forgotten among forgotten talk
The world is quite alone and it subsumes
the sucking sound of rain
through the gutters and the drains
glistening with apparitions
that skitter across the midnight
taking flight
as if some other night
perpetuated among the inanition
and still I hear the laughter which remains

The Glass Piano

In spring a strange pervasive smell persists,
life sprouts and quickly overtakes the earth,
recalling the roots of language to our midst,
fear organizes fevered jabberings
to meet the strange utility of sex.
Men walk outside of houses, mottled hues
of bright light flashing through windshaken leaves.
An infant's nose is pressed against the glass
to see dissolving motion as they pass,
like marks of crayon in a coloring book.
An oriole sits like a monument
upon a fountain, pecking at new life.
The kings an English grandmother recounts
possess no names or faces, flashing sounds
that till the earth, where glass keeps the wind out.
Who are the dead who lately walked the earth,
leaving their images on what remains,
peopling the leisure of more recent talk?
And still a strange pervasive smell persists,
countering the wind, and alienating rock.
Night comes. A castle sheds long celtic hair,
intoxicating the evaporate air,
and ideal spirits which are never there.
A hat rack stands unused inside a hall,
but peeped at on a constitutional,
visible through the grand, obstructive glass
of imperious houses, silent as we pass.
The author's house on the long country drive,
residual before we were alive,
fixes the morning with a pleasant stare.

But how do we know that we are really there,
and not some wheelbarrow rotting in the sun,
where gardeners like Socrates will come?
The jungle lashes woman to his man,
where poison orchids spread their inhuman plan.
Yet evening brings its after dinner sleep
in private clubs where members mustn't speak,
sprawling in armchairs with a newspaper,
dreaming of Cleopatra and Ben Hur,
strange portraits apparitions will concur,
waking to contorted puzzlements,
a low cacophony the learned stir.
Town meetings end, parting each councilor,
and still a strange pervasive smell persists,
hounding your footsteps, on the long walk home.
What force is rising up in all these things,
these pallid rejuvenations of the spring's?
Fear is all, uprising through the roots
of consciousness and language, to diffuse
broken perspectives irreconcilably,
substances nourishing the truly free.
In Boston the tall houses brightly lit
sleep impenetrable and separate.
Who hears the imprecations of these things?
A celtic maiden at her window sings,
calling to lovers who do not exist.

Meditations

It isn't really right
No, it really isn't fair
To compress and circumnavigate the night
To an image and a square
As still and motionless
As your just being there
And the circles should protest
That the light by which you're dressed
That the roundness of a sentence has expressed
That oblivion should be put to the test
Of other words used somewhere else
As if the clock at midnight up and tells
Of someone else
Of something else
And why behind its wings should the world hide
The sense of something it has held inside
And parting thus from all your memories
Still find your image here though ill at ease
Were there nothing to regret
Were the midnight newly met
And glowing grids stacked to eternity
Were all you see
This sense of someone else's sense of things
Dissipates and clings
To the silence that the hour brings
That's what we do
To make the hour new
And certainly not what we expect
But how then to inspect
The ethereal architect

Ben Mazer

Who clamours in the rose and gold
Of things when we are neither young nor old
Or to detect
The character of midnight when it fold
Into a map or set of chinese boxes
That have no say
In any increment of the world's way
So inconceivable it stands aloof
From the patter of the rain upon the roof
As idle as if one compelling truth
Were all we prayed for
Were all we stayed for
Shall I pass this to your hand
And receive the reprimand
Of one who came for
Of one who stayed for
The silence of the latching of a door
Or is there more
These meditations shake me to the core.

* * *

And the winter is so cold
The wind whips rain into a world that's old
And nothing stays
Beyond the worry and the strain of days
That end these ways
Accommodate some postulated stranger
To fortify the mind
That's left so much behind
And yet you'll find
That what is left can be distilled and strained

And left upon some lit but empty altar
Not yet to falter
But with resolve to seek and find
I've nothing in my mind
And cannot alter
The necessary change that you will find
Compels the world to which it is aligned
Folded, sealed and stamped and duly signed
By the serious exchequer
Of which we both concur
Merely to have passed the time
Severely to have made a rhyme
As savage as the midnight to a mime
Goes in repose
Out of all the gestures that he knows
And fixing there
A circle in the glowing of a square
No, it really isn't fair

Ben Mazer

Flat planes
Round planes
The night somewhere between
And all around
Sheds its gentle prayer to the rains
Till lifted quite
To the heroic stillness of the sight
What is not there
Currents with babbling laughter the empty square

The Glass Piano

The newspapers are rows of plotted fields
at breakfast, where the Admiral must go on
and please the heiress of the swords and shields.
The flowers are encroaching on the dawn.

Peace has come, the peace of cotton looms
and factories reopened. Peacetime cares
are blooming on the windowsills of rooms,
in gardens men projecting peacetime wares.

A steady hush grows like a symphony
to the cadenza of a potent rest.
The rivers soak the idle and the free;
keen eyes fix on the progress to the west.

But you and I do naught but sip our tea;
feeling each word's weight in eternity.

Ben Mazer

A black man sleeps inside a dusty cellar;
while people pass like minutes on the streets.
The universe is made of swards of color;
or darkness where rough hand on old pot beats.
A vision of the world is colored yellow
on someone's little childish book of birds.
The upper rooms are closed to real birds' hello;
and silence is enough to have of words.
Gaily the gate, the pram pushed past the park;
the semblances of shapes are bright and stark.
A man of standing leaves his sealskin mark
upon some Cromwell's picnic in the park.
The birds keep bankers' hours on the fence;
life is co-opted without recompense.

The Glass Piano

Lewis is dead. Retinal Imperialist,
too high for thunder, bodiless unpleased,
amidst the revocations of his order,
now clipped and faltered, mattes of forward-braizing
automatons, non-life released to heaven,
just as his stifling darkness swept each corner,
appearance shrinking to unconsciousness,
like one who stands in stairwell, midnight-mute,
fixing the conscience with its own high mirrors,
then disappears, to say not "as you were",
but "as you will be in full consciousness"
beyond the many grids stacked high to heaven,
each isolated window's feeble symbol,
to timelessness, beyond each gargoyle's sentry,
through looking-glass, to Alice and the Apes.
The Caliph needs new forms to build his city.

Ben Mazer

It was on a grey rainy day,
a grey rainy day within a grey rainy day,
a Saturday with nothing one needed to do,
that I went to the Old Vic in search of something new,
the devil of a woman's eyes of sparkling blue,
whirling with violence in entrechats nothing to eschew.
That was the first time that I laid eyes on you,
but soon the long coach ride through the Spanish planes at dawn
had spoiled my imperious plans; my patience was gone,
for art must be greater than anything or anyone,
and I cannot let anyone interfere with my plans,
least of all someone who I have chosen to dance,
through Lido, through Biarritz, through Venice, through France.
But Saturday, Saturday, thinking that you were crowned
with a rainy intimacy—but I was nowhere to be found.
I cursed myself in my office, and met with my men,
affecting indifference as to when I would see you again.
I, who would make you dance till life was gone.
Only the red shoes must live and linger on.
And here's the thing I understand about the rain:
that boundless joy must be dispersed in boundless pain.

The Glass Piano

Blown on the widow walk she holds
a distant prospect of the sea
within the figure that she moulds
of images that I shall see.
I could not think her lithe enough
to bury Cadmus in the clay,
but am intent upon the stuff
she sometimes turns to me to say.
It seems I'm needing of reform.
Babies give in to hands so warm,
warmth perpetrated by a scarf,
a fur collar on the wharf.
The terrace and the library
have books that, musty with salt air,
have been handled by presidents,
though at tea we hardly care.
I listen for my lessons,
and strive to meet the noble bloom
of time that shifts from stance to stance,
yet holds one honour in the room.
The sparkling rising of desire,
like champagne to the moon doth float,
in images of evening attire,
tuxedo, gown, and winter coat,
a gondolieri for the moat
that brings us to the rarest stars,
you tinkle with more liquid fires,
all glassy as the Hamilcars.
But when the calendar we cross,
for things to do, a show to see,

Ben Mazer

I count those days among my loss,
am borne up by this strange duress.
That you should not have come this far,
beyond the pavilion on the hill,
the end of the material,
the gloss of the ethereal
drizzling as hard as autumn rain,
upon an unspoken sort of pain,
one's familiarity with the city
dies just as hard of pity.

The Glass Piano

There is no perfect synthesis,
in the autumn's chrysalis,
streets are in a stellar hold,
the streets are windy, cold and old,
examined by the modern eye.
Someone opens a car door,
and all the world is in a rush,
despite the fact it's nearly four,
December in its stellar hush,
and will awake to bright and cold
mementos of another day.

Ben Mazer

Necesse est Perstare?

Twenty minutes after midnight. The houses sleep.
And in them the tales of ships, of clocks, of houses.
The tales of voyages, and the return to houses.
One after another,
one next to another, or attached to each other,
their different shapes, or same shapes,
bigger, smaller. Longer, wider. Taller windows. Shorter windows.
Loud and crowded, or empty and silent,
with a telephone, a car in the driveway or out front,
and places to sleep.
You walk out (if you are him)
into the October evening at a brisk pace
with a newspaper tucked under the arm of your Harris tweed
looking about chiefly at wind
blowing dried leaves blue white brown
into or out of ditches or onto trees
till they're a little wet,
it is true.
But you and I, we meet in rain,
where we can come in from the rain,
and have a sandwich, and a coffee.
They telephone each other,
on regal steps, fast and alert.
From one to another, string trees with lanterns,
to God above, the son of an old love.
Morning. The leg swings forward long and wide.
Mariana Pineda is no longer trapped inside.
A Columbia student now, eyes roam the brick facade
of an apartment building, in the land of Nod.
Keystone cornices replace the God.

The Glass Piano

A son of the Alhambra declines to pack a rod.
A generation, scarred by ghosts of war,
meets on street corners, each greeting as before.
The whole great mix has been to the theatre,
read the papers, interrogated the interlocutor,
in closets with incense, in kitchens with bathtub whiskey,
B. G. Brooks, Zoe Hawley, Viola Tree.
Up drives with radios, in uniform,
to telephones, each waiting for the forum
to isolate with definition their indecorum;
they greet on corners, in guttural voices, ailing,
jolly, with teeth and uteruses failing.
And speak one language, good for spring canoeing,
after long winters of Napoleonic rueing.
Necesse est perstare? This too will come,
later in summer to most, in spring to some.
The college widow deftly sidesteps a bomb.
The student union sounds the general alarm.
There is no lack of things to look and see,
of books to read, of points to ABC.
Only the still window, in the unwitnessed hall,
must be susceptible to anything at all.
And will greet guests, in winter and in fall.
Each couple knowing the same modern dances,
and how the judeo-christian world enhances
the pagan rituals and rites of spring
the voice trapped in a gramophone must sing.

Cracked faces, aligned in a vacant ring.

Cracked faces, to battle ancient come:

Ben Mazer

brick buildings rise to God—a vacant emporium.
While trains rush out into the provinces—
old ghosts the armour in the hall commences.

An After Dinner Sleep

Entering the open air summer movie theatre,
the hour after dinner, the sky grown dim,
some rustling heads bobbing to find their seats,
the lights come on the screen, the show begins,
displacing cares and attitudes of the day,
each one prepared for a personal fantasy,
the sudden change of scene, and you are in
Cairo, privy to an intimate conversation,
silence broken by the crackling of spoken words,
clipped and conspiratorial, lush in its ease,
settling down to a world of eternity,
where all repeats, and is forever there,
unchanging, after many a crowd, many a show,
to which the people nightly come and go,
leaving them there, these conversationalists
who never change, but dissemble unattached
in the cosmos as light and sound, electric charges
of being constituting their own drama,
vanishing in space but not in mind,
reminding us of the nature of our being.

Movies are ghosts that couldn't get around.
Trapped in a ray of light, a wave of sound,
a box of tubes, molecular ghosts flee
conditions atmospheric that surround
continuums of time and entity,
broadcast indentures of God's parity,
stirring the memory they feebly hound
with words and images that aren't there,
their afterglow that is so tightly wound

Ben Mazer

around the lurch and flux of stratosphere,
forgotten to be remembered where they stood,
parti-esoteric where most good
as individual fuel to meditate
the chasms of existence which abate.

Walk into the theatre five minutes late,
and hear the voices as you find your seat;
look up and you are in a photoplay,
a drawing room in Cairo or in Crete,
mid-conversation; catch the words they say,
their brittle echo through the theatre,
and settle in for a two-hour stay,
and try to understand what they aver:
they speak so fast, then dry, deliberate,
where missing walls extend out to the sky,
the dry hump of a hothouse crescent moon,
the wall-less proxy, the old family friend
who's always there when things begin or end,
wherefore his great need to be involved?
The panic of your dreams is slowly solved,
to sample dramas that extend elsewhere
to hieroglyphic myths with rumbling hair …
You hide the nazi, or you turn him in,
to let the ancient rituals begin,
Tiresias, who has foresuffered all,
a poster selling popcorn on the wall …
A bat will hover in the drawing room,
and orient the audience to doom
they might escape, but they will wait and see
the zeitgeist tested for alacrity …

The Glass Piano

then file out to their domesticity.

Out of the fog a certain voice is thrust,
like clip clop footsteps hovering over feet,
the opening audio of a photoplay,
where you come in to follow as you must,
Egyptian nights of aristocracy,
tapping their cigarettes against a case,
the close-up crackling of a newspaper,
an intimacy to which you defer,
relishing summer palms on winter nights,
like men who disappear into a club,
out of the fog into a library,
where silence is so thick that you can see
maidens undressing in silk negligees,
or exports on their landwards way to sea,
invisible interests in the provinces,
and fall to a dreaming after-dinner sleep.
The mountains thunder, and the seas are deep,
drenched with the images of ancient worlds,
a Chinese emperor's hospitality,
on the eve of travels, the profligacy
of fields of poppies, saffron, cardamom,
all threatened by the revolutionary bomb.
The shards of images, blistering, torturing
the mind, have left the Hampstead evening blind,
though turn into an alley as you might,
imposing doorways return you to your sight,
firm as the grave, brass knockers that confer
fragments of fear and peace where the rats stir,
until a voice awakens, "Good evening, sir."

Ben Mazer

Now the two sisters have returned to London.
If one is done, the other must be undone.
You strain your eyes through columns, chance to see
the early return of the Viscount-Marquis.
Your monthly pension takes you on a spree
to Biarritz, Bretagne, Brittany,
and you will not be back till early fall,
and then again might not return at all,
the garish drainpipes climbing up facades
all violently symbolic, and at odds
with simple pleasures countrysides bequeath
to girls with dandelions between their teeth.
There is no fiction that can firmly hold
the world afloat above the weight of gold,
but all your progress drains out to the lee
of million-fold eternal unity.

What is the charm of slippers to the stars,
the hammering rumble of the Hamilcars,
projecting all their mysteries to see
the chimney-pots spread out across the city,
and the slow box of incremental fires
merge kisses on the operatic stairs,
hidden so that even time can't see
the mumbling promises you made to me.
I read all night, my eye falls on the door
in silent shadows at the stroke of four.
The nymphs have left stray shawls upon the shore,
who urgently into the cabs had climbed,
in softer hours when brief love still rhymed.
Who shall unlock the eternal paradigm?

The Glass Piano

Laughter streams like rain across the cars,
stirs audibly the let out theatres,
where no other form of silence mars
the peace of ribboned letters thrust in drawers.
The ibis is in concord with the rain,
mosaic rivers, remote and Byzantine,
relieve the world, lift childhood from its pain,
whose process multiplies its fertile sign:
how to brick buildings the whole world can fall,
as if it never happened, as if all
had gathered in this room to gently sleep,
incognizant of promises to keep.
And whosoever shall redeem the squalls,
each rivulet which from the dark sky falls?

Germ sprung from a rock, a windy castle
returns to earth. The dry grass strains the wind
of cooling planets, a headless knight, germane
to April flowers springing from dry earth,
their numbers countless as air-flight manifests
that dot a century, Centurion.
This German seed of proto-indices,
atomic memory and stark component
of motion and of glottal utterances,
folds lightning in the ocean, breaks the mountains.
Not strictly grey or brown, the cardinal
exhumes slim shades of green that break the earth.
Seeds fly through air, and taper like a ghost
among the querulous, germinal and moist,
the apparitions of old savoire faire.
A windy springing, germinal, germane,

to monstrous waves washed on the wasted plain.
Tall waves of blade-whirl take all men again
as Hokusai envisioned, turned to rain.
Erected castles, bilious suburban gain
the poet's eye sweeps in his lofty pain,
travelling far above the orphaned roofs,
no vocable but the component grain
to settle all the sleepers in his proofs,
component vocable that can't be split
where all dramatic situations sit.
Our German is the philologic core
of indic madness, mystery, and more.
Germ sprung from rock, a windy Elsinore.

One cannot assess the force that drives the rain,
if driving thus into the heart of pain
the recent past endows a partial stain
on the whole present. Crosswinds cannot solve
what crowds that drift into the rain revolve
around the present, too soon to resolve
the forces extant, thoughts the wind sprang
up to serve humanity from culture's cup
the dying light on which the victors sup.
Nothing sheds nothing. Whole particular
world cognizances suffer to aver
the wind wrought eyes the rain will wet and blur,
too soon too late. We are not what we were!
While god alone will scale and fill us up.

Unreality is not pushed back,
but like a fiction emerges, unreferenced

except in qualities or sense-data,
unverifiable in their own closed systems.
This is enough to posit they are true,
or in some sense neither true nor false,
but welcome enough, for their indications.
Take for example two ends of a street,
from one end which (and which end is it really)
out of the London fog our man emerges,
a complex of unbound hallucinations,
of uncompleted bearings or desires
that can't account for outside precedence.
Why should the dream not murder the real man,
or seem to do so, if but fractionally,
as if to say I've read of it what I can,
when there's no reader but in lucubrations.

A brown fog wraps as it will seem to do
around the armchair and the lofty view,
with yellow light that penetrates the ceilings
uncertain of its basis in the feelings,
but focused on a yellow text of page
that rises up in Sanskrit to the age
of Lanman's Harvard Oriental Series
and modern philosophic notes and queries.
How wide the margins, blocking from all view
all but the virgin snows of Waterloo,
the type like armour standing in the hall
that makes you think of anything at all,
where disconnected from October night,
dead through dead branches vacant wind takes flight,
germane anticipation of the snows

to which all speculation surely goes,
firm and abrupt as the Hapsburg empire
finds only vacant agents left to sire.
An after-dinner dream! Surely to sleep
the Buddha's fire sermon falls so deep
it is not wakened by the telephone,
or windy castles, or a vacant bone,
but stands evaporate in the March air,
germinal, not counting any there,
and speeds across the rooftops of the village,
in search of ideal innocence to pillage.

A rare edition floundered in its state,
the words dreamed over fed the seven seas
with passages, the cosmos conjugate,
bereft and baffled, of disparate entities …
Dr. Cyriax sitting on the bridge,
who counts the lights go out, obstructs a star
from sinking to her cabin, very far
from where the last transmission throws its switch …
These others in their beds prepare for dawn,
but in the streets the London fog goes on,
past ceilings higher than the eyes can see,
reflexive light of pure staticity …
The Dr. is impressed with what we learn,
and counts the distant panels as they burn …

Before you awaken into consciousness,
you may have some vague memory of this:
a garden, loosely bounded, in the sun,
to which the archer and the gardener come,

The Glass Piano

a statue of Cromwell standing undisturbed,
inhuman innocence that's unperturbed;
and you may meet Goliath in the shed,
among the worms disturbing the frost's bed.
A sundial tells you all you need to know:
of vital noon, a barrow, and a spade,
a berry-laden bush bristling in shade,
the calendars old apparitions made,
where galaxies of dust are lightly laid
on shelves while all are sleeping, and the maid
has not materialized this morning yet,
where wars of memory settle till they're set
in night's cool meditations, a penny ante bet.
How can we climb to see the latest show,
the silence Europe's soaked with what we know,
the ravaged Orient that bursts to blow?
We lay in beds, and watch the headlights pass
along the walls, across the frame of glass
that covers up a clown's face, painted rose,
through depths of living which each person knows.

Symphonic dull varieties of green
animating with a classic spleen
each dangling berry focusing the scene,
the chessboard motives of inhuman voice
simplifying the surrounding noise
of splashing youths with allegoric choice,
the trireme of the sun, the wind, the sheen
of rippling image, one fondly silent threne,
while Socrates, philosopher no more,
almost historian, stands at the door

of webs and teacups, lyric fantasies
that draw the crowd to scaled eternities ...
attention to the situation, scene
of every choice transformed by what has been ...

1940s Middlebury symphonic clown
green green green green green
swirl the trees by the luscious pool
tympani breezes rotswort towering
shaved limbs conductor affixes
to Plato and caves and frames
Socrates famous for saying hello
masturbating in the center of the meadow
while night sleeps in slithering marble
occasionally a passing headlight's glow
but there is no philosophy here
but only
the tapping before the orchestra begins
and the bathers in their emerald tight skins
who know from an accent that you have come a distance.

Webster transposed to an attic. Orange alcove glows.
A tree leans. Light sweeps its leaves
like wind or rain. The window lets in a little view.
How we hump and toss our memories
in comfort there. Silence like talk flows,
tossed by the wind or rain, swept by the light,
tossed cool. An ancient stage direction stirs
a bit of speech, jumbled in modern tongue.
What do we wait for? Who are we waiting for?
In torpor languishing like wind or rain

we toss our memories. A bit of speech stirs,
breaking the silence, and correcting rain,
as if to say, "I was expecting you."
So much to think. So much to do.
The city spreads out various from here,
adjacent to our seclusion's wider sphere.

Sudden appearance: that's epiphany.
A world that comes from nowhere is the world.
Slinking around corners along the sidewalk squares,
in mornings that are oblivion: that's the world.
They come to our attention: nubs of twisted steel
lovers maneuver around. Are they us?
Are they us to be so large and fill the world:
inceptions which are immense: eternity.
The mind blocks out so much, that it can see.
Then rain comes, punishing the evening roofs,
and hurrying progress, so blind and inert.
A cab's closed door—prelude, a change of scene.
The downpour buries lovers in their love:
slinking away to what has never been.

No recollection in the art nouveau wood
stirs them to action; a roof of trees inside
their ingrown sickness is enough and good
for clatter of teacups; some may feign to hide,
fooling themselves, but not go unobserved
by doctors' rushing inactivity,
the least of hope, that justice will be served,
doubting their secrecy's insanity.
Some recognize a mother, or a sister,

returning to threats of doctors' cruelty,
their unburst fears to carry like a blister,
their nemesis personal continuity.
For to know fraud, cures of the charlatans,
have stood at doors, on beaches more than once,
thinking escape must mean the fatal pounce,
as diagnoses slip through traitors' hands.

Go back to that day. The shadows thick
with seeing by the Chanford Arms.
The colors brilliant as a day in May.
Our eyes alert as if we had been sick,
noticed inscriptions carved into the brick.
Easy and voluble, slow to make our way,
we set out, and although we richly dreamed,
we never dreamed that we would come to harms.
We were preoccupied with how things seemed,
and how their seeming, broken into bits,
made up life's flux in all its starts and fits.
We talked your childhood out a country mile.
Night: twentieth-century man in a turnstile,
recording images, marking the blurs of form
that keep each in his solitude from the storm;
we passed beneath the windows thickly lit
with fleeting scenes, that were the whole of it:
the whole of man, alone, and quite unknown,
scenes never changing, though the years be gone.
Happy to be as brilliant as two stars
that soared above the earth, and looking down
at all the tinkling lights of homes and cars,
in voices booming as the Hamilcars

remarked ourselves, then gently turned towards home.
By-passing every strict familiar sight
and obverse of the odyssey of night.
The gallery of unalterable fires.
Lit up, yes, but in the end quite slight.

He looked around and saw what he liked best,
and he prepared his own Octoberfest.
The winds were grey, which blew like billowed clouds,
beneath which he discerned among the crowds,
the missing forms of many lit-up shrouds:
a grocer helpful in Thanksgiving rain,
a wall street banker waiting for the train.
The headlines of the newspapers averred
a unified delight in the deferred
long hour of homecoming. All were heading home:
by days, and hours, changes at railway stations,
out to the provinces, with a little patience.
He closed his book, and leaned back in his seat,
and saw the thousand images repeat.
For him there never could be going home.
There was the eucharist. There was the poem.

Afterword

BEN MAZER INTERVIEWED BY ROBERT ARCHAMBEAU

RA: I'd like to begin with process. Often, poets have spoken of their process as one or another kind of mixture of deliberation and intuition—whether they call the intuitive element "the muses" or (in Jack Spicer's case) a radio transmission from Mars. How does a poem begin for you, and what happens once you have the initial impulse?

BM: Jack Spicer was deeply in love with the relatively unknown but deeply brilliant poet Landis Everson, who in turn, late in his life, fell deeply in love with me, so I not only know all of the Spicer literature, but have heard many intimate, off-the-record stories of Jack's thinking about poetry, and his methods of composition. Like many of the best poets, he was possessed by words, and his poems came to him as voices that he heard and recorded without any other guidance than long, elaborate and strenuous preparations for being able to write poems—when they came into his head—which must have acted as a kind of net or formal conception already deeply ingrained in his consciousness by the time he was struck by inspiration, instinct, and intuition—what he referred to as transmissions from Mars—so that the poems were deeply guided by a well-prepared consciousness, with its fully digested lore and ideas, and personal feelings concomitant with his own rather compendious knowledge in many intellectual areas, such as philosophy, as well as the knowledge that comes with personal experience, while at the same time being completely intuitive and unexpected events of inspiration. I think most poets of a high calibre work in this way to some degree or other—typically hearing first lines of poems simply come into their head, sometimes even as heard voices, successively followed by a flow of words, lines, and passages that come as naturally as leaves to a tree, and are imbued with what Eliot called the auditory imagination, a deeper level of meaning that is not contained in the literal meaning of the words, but—on another level—in the sounds of the words, their origins and accumulated meanings and resonances, and their emotional suggestivity, until the poem peters out, completes itself, and the poet knows it. Sometimes the poet goes on too long—maybe just a line or two beyond the point where the genuine inspiration ends—but the poet is quick to spot this dead wood and snip it off to give the poem the wholeness and unity that it must have. There are many descriptions—throughout the history of poetry—of poets, many of them of the greatest stature—creating poetry in exactly this way.

I find that this is precisely the way I work when I am writing my best poems—that they are miracles of inspiration and intuition, and typically begin with a first line simply coming into my head—something like hearing a voice that fully forms itself without my interference—and then followed by another, and another, and so forth. I do, and I imagine other poets do this also, to a certain extent, realizing what the meaning of the inspiration is, even if only intuitively, tend to offer it a little guidance through an act of intense concentration on where I know the poem must lead, or upon some symbolic image or emotion (what Eliot called significant emotion), which I know instinctively to be the heart of the poem, and which I know must be unravelled to its end, even if I don't quite, at least consciously, know what that end is. I am there to find out what the end is, and I must seek the path the poem beckons me down in order to find out. This does occasionally demand a tiny bit of interference on my part: a search for the right word to convey what I feel to be the object of my attention; an intensified focus—more meditative and open than merely conscious—on the object of attention; a determination to get some nuance of what I discover to be the meaning or quality of the emotional experience of the poem *into* the poem. But I possess a well-prepared machine or instrument, and largely when real inspiration hits there is very little or often no need whatsoever for interference on my part. The best poems simply write themselves, with a minimum of this sort of interference, and I imagine many people would be surprised to learn that internal rhyme, end rhyme, and meter come to me without conscious thought or guidance of any kind on my part—they are simply what the poem itself wants to say; and I am often surprised myself to discover afterwards how many connections and meanings and levels of meaning a poem which the unconscious created can possess due to what is essentially the gift of a possession of a naturally musical and meaningful consciousness which has paid its dues in experience and preparation. The most exciting poems of all are those in which I am swept up entirely by a cascading ocean of words which seem punched through with an infinite number of levels of meaning, all deeply felt in the act of composition, and which are above all deeply resonant musical conveyances of significant emotion. My long poem "Divine Rights" (in my collection *Poems*) is an example of this. Another is a poem from the same collection, "The Double".

To put it an entirely other way: the advanced poet is likely to know exactly what he is doing, and is unlikely to make a mistake, even when writing without thought and by intuition. He is like a jazz musician in that he either is on target and gets it right the first time, or else he flubs it, in which case he may wish to simply scrap the entire take as not up to snuff. Revision is largely, for me, a matter of cutting a line, finding a single better word (sound being the operative principle as much as the literal level of meaning), scrapping a weakening stanza, or some such minor alteration. Consider the fact that revision is as much an improvisatory act as the original act of composition, and depends just as much on inspiration and intuition. When the poet is at the height of his powers, revision is often if not generally entirely unnecessary.

RA: On the question of revision—you've lavished considerable attention on the poetry of John Crowe Ransom, even editing his collected poems in an edition that includes all of the revisions he made over time. For you, is revision something that comes immediately after composition? Ransom would revisit old poems many years later, often changing them significantly. Is that something you've been tempted to do?

BM: I've never been tempted into the kind of forays into compulsive, perpetual revision that absorbed Ransom late in life, though who is to say what devil might get into me when I reach those later years. No, generally revision is as I've described in my answer to the first question: it is a very minor affair, and generally does come almost immediately after composition, if at all. When I write poems I have a great conviction about them when I feel I am doing it correctly (that is, in the way that suits me, and suits the object of my mental attentions), and generally I tend to feel I have got it right the first time. If one is going to get it right at all, why not be done with it at the first stroke of the anvil. When I am writing I have that kind of control over my instrument, again like a jazz musician who has trained himself in the art of improvisation and concentration. When I am on, I am on, and I know it, and I know that I can do anything that the poem wants me to do. The poems that don't work out, the false starts, and half-successful attempts, I simply toss into the dustbin. It is easy to see in those poems that the poetry was not really genuine. I try to explain this to people: if, when it comes, it is genuine poetry, it is not going to need to be altered. It is just the case that I have prepared my instrument particularly well and thoroughly. Others may need to proceed more slowly, more cautiously, and refine over time; that is not my method. If I make a mistake, I feel I may as well give up for the day. I have a great trust in the powers of the unconscious to present one with gifts of treasure in the realm of significant utterance, even if that utterance is not immediately accessible to total comprehension. Eliot famously told Richards that he felt his most successful poems were those which elicited the most various and unexpected array of interpretations, strange and foreign to the poet's own understanding of his poem.

This is a sign of the mysteries. It is the poem that rules and has authority over the poet, and not the other way around. The poet is the conduit for the poem. Otherwise we would just be writing what we already know. And even when we have a reason to write what we already know, sometimes especially when we have a reason to write what we already know, it is possible to get it right the first time, and still for the poem to be imbued with unexpected and rich meanings that the poet was not fully conscious of during the act of composition, though he is likely to notice them later. It is all a matter of the poet's capacity for concentration, and of his responsiveness to the powers of the unconscious mind.

Revision? Sometimes I'll work on a poem for several days in a row, as I did when I wrote the 41 sonnets in "The King" (*New Poems*); here's a case where composition itself is an act of revision through a process of accumulation. All composition is revision, just as all revision is composition.

RA: What can you tell us about the ways you prepare yourself to receive the poems when they come? To steal a phrase from Yeats, what is your singing school?

BM: Three things. One, about thirty years of continuous reading in every area of literature, with a continuous application to poetry and the criticism of poetry, and foraging forays into philosophy, history, anthropology, psychology, popular culture, family lore, love itself, and other subjects as well. Two, many years of hard labour scanning meters and cadences and other technical minutia of the most accomplished verse one can find, coupled with unceasing attempts to master the art of writing rhymed and metrical verse until it becomes effortless and as natural as breathing, so that one can break from or depart from or transmogrify these things at will or whim with authority, control and meaning. Three, intensive exercises in the arts of memory and concentration, with particular attention to the knack of holding an emotional memory steady in the mind's eye. There is also the fact of one's background. I was particularly lucky in this, in that I was surrounded by good books and a family that paid close attention to matters of aesthetic philosophy (whether they were aware of this or not!). But honestly, I think at root that it is an innate predisposition to deep reflection that one is born with, or in some cases scared or scarred into. My "singing school" is something like an adherence and receptivity to the ways and purposes of a controlling god. My source is divinity. Or perhaps it is the art of being transfixed to the point of solipsism. But with the object of focus the known world. There is more, but I can't recall what it was. I was six years old. I saw them through the window. The guys in the blue coats fired on the guys in the red coats, and then they all ran away.

RA: We've been talking about process, now I wonder if we can relate it to form. I know you have an affection for rhyme: one of the pleasures of visiting the Boston area is hearing you and Philip Nikolayev improvising rhymes together as you walk the little streets around Harvard Square. But rhyme in your work tends to be intermittent rather than regular, and you've never been affiliated with New Formalism. What attracts you about rhyme, and what role does it play in your poetry? Also, what can you tell us about other unusual features of your poetry—the sometimes irregular syntax, the deliberate use of British spellings, the way a sentence can sometimes meander. The latter feature accounts, I think, for the comparisons sometimes drawn with John Ashbery, although I know you don't see him as a major influence.

BM: I am amused and intrigued by rhyme, especially intricacies such as partial or near rhyme, assonance, and internal rhyme, which my work naturally seems to gravitate towards. It is quite unconscious, and comes from years of reading and hearing the sounds of poems and language in my head. I rarely set out to write a rhymed poem—though sometimes I do, with the purpose of attaining a sort of formal integrity that might aptly suit my subject matter when my subject matter is largely tonal: the rhymes, both internal and at line ends, come quite naturally and unconsciously, without my thinking about them. I'm heavily schooled in blank verse, Marlowe, and so forth, so—as in Lowell's late sonnets—you get a varied mixture of real rhyme, heavy rhyme, sporadic rhyme, and blank verse punctuated by occasional rhyme. I like it! It rings the ear with emotion and pleasure when it hits home and has *qualities*. Sometimes it echoes a cadence I have heard somewhere that must be in the back (or at the tip?) of my mind. This can raise poetic ghosts, and induce resonances with emotional significance. And yes, Philip and I have had many a long session of improvising perfectly rhymed sonnets for sheer pleasure's sake—it's sort of a running theme with us. Again, it all comes from taking apart poems for years as you would take apart a radio and put it back together again just to see how it worked: the lesson sticks with you. I played classical piano as a child, and jazz music growing up, so it is all music and indicative tonality to me. Sometimes when I listen to people talk all I hear is the rhyme; I must have a look on my face as though I'm in outer space. I wasn't aware that my poetry had irregular syntax in it—but I suppose that's because I'm forging an idiom that correlates directly with whatever it is I'm expressing, whatever perception or emotion (the two can be the same). It has struck me that my use of internal rhyme is quite innovative, in fact: something I wait for people to notice and gather in cafes to discuss. As to the syntax though, I have read far too much Hart Crane, and perhaps that has something to do with it, as well as my early obsession with Cubism, which breaks up the syntax of visual perception, color and shape. It is all emotionally correlative. I follow the thought, the emotion; what happens as a result to the language is my business, but *not* my business, if you see what I mean. The British spellings: my maternal grandmother was English, and I grew up on English literature as a child; I can't really say what attracts me to the British spellings; just the offbeat pleasure of it, I suppose. It's my nod or tip of the hat to English literature and culture; my turning away from the downgraded cultural atmosphere of our times. I also misspell words and have no wish to correct them! I feel I am stuck with the emotional and musical baggage of their peculiar semi-neological resonances, and can't betray them for a correct word. Joyce of course carried this to the extremes of obsession. Meandering: I suppose by that you mean largely tour-de-force enjambment, which has always struck me as the sign of genuine (the personally unique taking part in the universal) emotion in all the glory of its flux and flow: its *stasis* which has its simultaneous existence as well, as a rounded unity, or a pervasive extension, mirroring the nature of reality such as we come to know it in our more observant, less impinged upon moments. *Lycidas* is a famous example of how far you can take that (Ransom has a good essay on this in *The World's Body*); but of course it can always be pushed farther, and it is experience that does it. It's that contained flowing which is so universal, like the bounded and boundless sea, interminable rain, infinity without cessation (passion and reverence), one's movements through the world and through oneself, monumental archetypes of catastrophe and rebirth, the night. No, I don't see Ashbery as an influence at all. I like his stuff—it always amuses me, and I'm attracted to "The Skaters"—but it's not a model I would aspire to, or anything I would want to steal from for my own use. He's merely there, Ashbery. I drove by Sodus recently. I like that neck of the woods. Nice to think of young Ashbery emerging from such a place. Seriously, though, the comparisons with Ashbery drive me crazy. I see no resemblance whatsoever, other than some vague resonance of the Harvard outsider poetry tradition, which I, too, partook of. The parti-colored brick and cobblestone, and the grey sky over Mem Hall, kind of seep into you like damp weather in the autumn. Probably comes from a mutual love of French poetry and music, Apollinaire and Debussy and so forth, as well. And the historical moment (which I reject, in order to embrace). Someone said we are a late blooming generation. But whatever we are doing, it strikes me that we are making it new. The young crowd in ascendancy now has much to buck against. Why not simply follow one's own inspiration? And let the rest take care of itself. Oh, the syntax: it might come from layered and abrupt shifts in imagery and meaning. The cinematic quality of consciousness. I try to mirror my thought, or perhaps go further than that. A guy's alone. The skeleton of a horse is crossing an abandoned railway bridge. Everything in the world is in its place. But what is that but hunks of color: solipsism or divinity? Or both?

More about the syntax: Sometimes planes shoot off at oblique angles. Other planes shoot off at oblique angles from those planes, and others from those. This is the way the mind works: holding perception at a distance to the point of substitution. How else are we going to deal with the richness of our memories?

RA: It's interesting that you mention a "Harvard outsider tradition," since for most people the words "Harvard" and "insider" go together, like little cucumber sandwiches and summers in the Hamptons. What can you tell us about this tradition, and your relation to it?

BM: Poets are poets. You can't change them. They say nothing, stare into space, or talk like maniacs about incomprehensible complexities, and sometimes disappear for days on end without anyone ever finding out where they went. They procrastinate, and can't be made to do anything but read endless numbers of poetry books. They don't fit in socially at the Fly Club, they dress funny and don't know how to assert themselves, and are shunned by all but the strangest of social outsiders. This is as true at Harvard as any place, and probably even more true at a place like Harvard, where people are being groomed to be presidents and so forth. Practical concerns are not their forte. I'm third generation Harvard myself, but the Mazers were all Jewish (my grandfather Moses was class of '24, when there was still a quota, and there were, I think, no more than 8 to a dozen Jews at Harvard at most). I got into Harvard through the back door, as it were, as a Special Student (an offbeat status which I share with Robert Frost, Wallace Stevens, and Eugene O'Neill), and then only because Seamus Heaney and William Alfred (Robert Lowell's friend) wrote letters on my behalf. This was all contrived so that I could study with Seamus Heaney, but I took advantage of the situation and took courses with such excellent professors as Derek Pearsall (Chaucer), David Perkins (lyric poetry), Leo Damrosch (American poetry), and Donald Bacon (modernism), and was tutored privately by Bill Alfred. The literary studies at Harvard were brilliant at the time (many people were still alive who had known Eliot, Richards, etc.)—I don't know what they are now. I absorbed myself in them completely, and felt that I was entering a tradition. They were every last one of them outsiders: Tuckerman, Eliot, Frost, Stevens, Cummings, Wheelwright, Robert Lowell, Delmore Schwartz, Dunstan Thompson, Frank O'Hara, John Ashbery ... They were spooky ghosts on the fringes of that cucumber-sandwich crowd, and never the twain did meet. Few did well in their studies (Eliot was mediocre as an undergraduate), and many dropped out, or were thrown out. Delmore Schwartz surprisingly won the Boylston Prize for a brilliant philosophical essay in 1936. I've written about this before at length in *Fulcrum* (#5, 2006), where I think I summed up the situation of the outsider tradition pretty well, so perhaps it's best to wrap up this question with a passage quoted from my essay there:

"It is in fact precisely the poet, more than anyone, who has usually found himself to be problematic and institutionally marginal at Harvard, and who has typically had an unpredictable, unconventional relationship with the university. [...] By and large, the best of the Harvard poets have been far from either staid or academic. They have been poets, with all the wildness and sensitivity that that implies. What distinguishes them as Harvard poets or near Harvard poets—as often as anything—is a consciousness of

The Glass Piano

the tribulations—fugitive, obscure and various—of those who have existed with them in a continuous tradition: not Harvard's, but poetry's."

RA: Finally, I wonder if you could say a little something about the place and meaning of poetry in the world. You've been bold enough to speak publicly about the future of poetry: what do you see for poetry when you look in your crystal ball?

BM: I discovered Rimbaud when I was 16. I had played hookey from school and taken the bus into Harvard Square. In the basement of a very filthy used bookstore, I found an old blue and grey Pelican paperback anthology of French poetry and slipped it unnoticed into my pocket. It was a very grey, foggy, and sort of misty or rainy day, typical New England, and on the bus ride back I happened to have my eye caught by this poet, Jean-Arthur Rimbaud, who had been about my age when he had written his poems. I began reading and was immediately transported into some realm that I had never experienced before, but which I had the sensation of having always known had existed. It seemed as if words were detached from time and space. I didn't know Rimbaud was a famous poet, and I thought that this was my own discovery entirely, something that no one else in the world knew about except me. Right then and there I recognized that this fellow *was me*, and had written exactly what I was trying to write. I became insatiably obsessed, and I think that right there that was some kind of beginning, or a further beginning built upon other pivotal reading experiences of childhood such as my discoveries of Lewis Carroll, Poe, the perfectly circular sentences of Raymond Chandler, and the clipped and projective syntax of Samuel Beckett, whose *Waiting for Godot* I had dipped into with a sense of wonder and discovery. Among poets, Rimbaud was my first true hero. I thought that I possessed an immense secret about an entirely unknown figure. Through me, I felt, this person was living again. Ah, the providential reader! Years later, when I discovered the *Confessions* of Verlaine on the interminable hold shelf of an antiquarian book store, a book that was never for sale, and which I wasn't even allowed to look at until the owner had left the shop for the day, and the girl behind the counter took pity on me, I almost died of grief when I read, only at the very end of the book, that Rimbaud had just come into Verlaine's life, the only mention of him in the book's very last sentence. Why couldn't the *Confessions* have gone on! I tried to trace Rimbaud's footsteps in the snow around Harvard Square—and almost succeeded!

I guess what I'm driving at is that poetry and poets are for poetry and poets, and only then for the rest of the world to catch up with, or be stirred by in some way that it can't quite fully comprehend. Poetry has an endless future, in a way encompassing the entire universe, but I think that the core of the thing, when you get right down to it, is that, aside from writing sheerly for his or her self, a loved one, a poet friend, or truth or God (however fictional the poet's means), the poet is really writing for the providential reader, that strange young person of the far distant future, who, with immensely empathic consciousness, will stumble across the stuff and say to himself, "This person is me."

OCTOBER 2015

Acknowledgments

Poems in this collection have appeared in *Raritan, The Battersea Review, Fulcrum, Spoke, The Ocean State Review, Scarriet, Plume, MadHat Review, E-Verse Radio, Open Letters Monthly,* and *The Philadelphia Review of Books*. The interview with Robert Archambeau first appeared in *Eyewear*.

Ben Mazer

About the Author

BEN MAZER was born in New York City in 1964, and educated at Harvard, where he studied with Seamus Heaney, and the Editorial Institute, Boston University, where his advisors were Christopher Ricks and Archie Burnett. His collections of poems include *White Cities* (Barbara Matteau Editions, 1995), *Poems* (The Pen & Anvil Press, 2010), *January 2008* (Dark Sky Books, 2010), *New Poems* (The Pen & Anvil Press, 2013). He is the editor of *The Collected Poems of John Crowe Ransom* (Un-Gyve Press, 2015), Hart Crane's *The Bridge: The Uncollected Version* (MadHat Press, 2015), *Selected Poems of Frederick Goddard Tuckerman* (Harvard University Press, 2010), and Landis Everson's *Everything Preserved: Poems 1955–2005* (Graywolf Press, 2006), which won the first Emily Dickinson Award from the Poetry Foundation. He lives in Cambridge, Massachusetts, and is the editor of *The Battersea Review*.

www.ingramcontent.com/pod-product-compliance
Lightning Source LLC
Chambersburg PA
CBHW020356170426
43200CB00005B/189